BISHOP L. J. COPPIN

UNWRITTEN HISTORY

BY

BISHOP L. J. COPPIN

111601

NEGRO UNIVERSITIES PRESS

NEW YORK

Reprinted in 1968
by Negro Universities Press
A DIVISION OF GREENWOOD PUBLISHING CORP
New York

Library of Congress Catalogue Card Number: 68-55878

Printed in the United States of America

PREFACE

———

Intermingled with this "Unwritten History" is the story of my life. Being all from memory, except here and there the verification of a date, there may be some repetitions. Of course much of the "Story" is omitted, but, things that impressed me most, and facts that seem to me most important among the "Unwritten" things, are noted. Those who are fond of reading novels about men who never lived, and things that never did and never will happen, may enjoy a change to something that is historic and real. If the example of some of the worthy ones mentioned inspires some-one else, the object of the author is accomplished.

CONTENTS

———

UNWRITTEN HISTORY

CHAPTER I.

Birth and Boyhood.

It was at Frederick Town, Maryland. Be sure and distinguish between Frederick in Western Maryland, and Frederick Town on the Eastern Shore.

It makes all the difference in the world to an Eastern Shore man. You may call the difference only sentimental, but Frederick Douglass was born there. To be sure, Benjaman Banneker was born on the Western side of the famous Chesapeake Bay.

Perhaps Bishop A. W. Wayman more than any one else, advertised the Eastern Shore as the "Garden Spot of the World."

It is indented with rivers that flow into the Chesapeake Bay. These rivers are full of fish, oysters and crabs. At some points along the

Bay, the fishing and crabbing are perennial.
Shad, and herring in the Spring; crabs, hard
and soft shell, in the Summer; oysters in the
Winter, and fish of various kinds the year
'round.

All of the "Eastern Shore" is not in Maryland. Virginia claims a part of this modern
"Promised Land." So, the expression goes;
"the Eastern Shore of Maryland and the
Eastern Shore of Virginia," with Maryland
always first; for the collossal figure of Frederick Douglass in Maryland is bound to loom
up.

Frederick Town is on the Sassafras river,
the boundary line between the counties of
Kent and Cecil—English names.

This little stream, as clear as crystal, forms
the Southern boundary of Cecil, the northern-
most county on the Eastern Shore.

Frederick Town, once an active lumber and
grain market, nestles on the banks of the Sassafras, just five miles from its head, where is
a town known as "Head of Sassafras," made
more or less famous by the grist mill that
stands, or stood—at the falls, where the rushing waters tumble into the river, after turning
the mill wheel day and night. Upper Cecil
and Kent patronize this mill for miles around.

Some of my earliest and most pleasant recollections are, of going with "Billy Cannan" to "Freemans Mill." We drove the big black horse, Jim, when we did as we were told. He was blind in one eye, "as big as a barrell" as round as an apple, and as fat as butter. A kind and safe driving horse for boys, and as fine a saddle horse as there ever was in "Sassafras Neck." But if we boys could catch the old man King "napping" we would hitch up Dandy, a fine looking spirited bay, and slip away to the mill.

Opposite Frederick Town, Cecil County, is Georgetown, Kent County. These were rival grain markets.

Sailing crafts plied the river from both sides with grain, principally wheat and corn, from early fall until the river became frozen over. In mid-summer, the Delaware and Chesapeake Canal steamers would come up for peaches. Besides these, a flat bottom side wheel steamer ran every summer between Frederick Town and Baltimore, sixty miles away, carrying passengers and light freight to the merchants, country store keepers, of Galena and George-Town of Kent, and Cecilton and Frederick Town of Cecil; and passengers back and forth.

These boats looked large to me. They were the first I ever saw. I went on one of them, a sailing craft, to Baltimore when about seven years of age. Baltimore was the first city I ever saw. Our goodly ship (?) dropped anchor in the busy Patapsico river, amid scores and scores of steam and sailing crafts, river boats, coast wise and ocean steamers, and ships and brigs, and tugs. What a sight to a pair of young country eyes! Three score years, as full as they have been of travel and sight seeing, have not been sufficient to obliterate the scenes of the Patapsico harbor, nor to wipe out the impression made, upon my first visit there.

My mother took me there. A wonderful mother! Great men are not the only men who have great mothers. Some obscure men who have not been much more known in the world's great movements, than a match that starts a blaze and immediately perishes, have also had great mothers.

The light of John the Baptist was cruelly blown out before he saw the fruit of his labor; but, the Kingdom he proclaimed is still marching on. St. Luke tells us about his mother.

We know about the mother of Moses, and Timothy and Samuel, and John Wesley and others; but, there are unknown mothers whose sons, breathing their spirit, inheriting their nobility of soul, and becoming the heirs and beneficiaries of their faith and prayers, have helped to make up "the salt of the earth," both upon the mountain top of fame, and in the vale of obscurity.

There were seven of us children, four boys and three girls. The most of us were born "on the hill" in Frederick Town.

Abraham Lincoln gave character to the log cabin. When ex-Vice President Fairbanks died—June, 1918, the Press referred to him as "the last of the famous Log Cabin Statesmen."

Since America's most famous could come from log cabins, it has become popular to refer to these primitive dwelling places of earth's lowly, as a birth place. All the same, this is not the way of the world's desire, preferably.

We speak of a mother's love, but mothers have instinct also. Perhaps it is inspired vision.

What is it that could make a mother persist in clandestinely having her child taught to read and write when there was no visible prospect whatever of it ever being of service to him; and, besides, when, it being in violation of the law, it could only be done at a peril.

My maternal grandmother was free born, while her husband, Perry Lilly, was a slave. Alas! a slave! A slave in a country whose citizenship was made up of those who fled from oppression, and fought, and bled, and died for liberty!

Children took the condition of their mother. This was the surest way to perpetuate slavery where the masters were so plentifully the fathers. For this reason many a slave man married a free woman, that his children might be free.

Many slave men, veritable heroes, purchased their freedom by working by day for their masters, and by night for themselves; hiring their time, etc.

Many a free man married a slave woman because he loved her, and purchased her and her children.

My grandmother being free, the Lilly children were free born, and John Coppin, also free born, married Jane, one of the Lilly girls.

There was a large family of them; all girls but one. They got the reputation of being the best girls in the neighborhood, and my

Aunt Clara told me that they called themselves "the Shoestring Breed."

The girls all married free men, and grandfather, Perry Lilly, was "set free" before the Emancipation, on account of meritorious service. But he was about through serving by that time anyway.

His wife Amelia, had passed away, and he had a few years left to enjoy life with his children and grandchildren. I remember the visit he made to our home. I do not remember my grandmother.

The parentage of my father is not so easily traced. I do not, even now, see many Coppins in the directories and 'phone books.

In a visit to Covington, Kentucky, when Editor of the A. M. E. Review, I saw on a sign over a large store: "John Coppin." That was my father's name. I had never seen or heard of it outside of the family. I immediately went in and asked for "Mr. Coppin," and purchased a souvenir from the store.

In a rather lengthy conversation with him, for we became interested in each other, on account of the name, he gave me some facts about the history of the name. He said it was of German origin, and was primarily Coppenger. Coming to England the "ger" was

dropped.   Coming to America the "en" was
changed to "in," or "pen" to "pin," thus Coppin.

As soon as he told me that, I began to account for the friendship, peculiar friendship
that existed between our family and the only
Coppins I ever knew outside of our family.
James Coppin, a white man, was a bachelor,
with one sister, Araminta. She married Robert
Price. I think now that she and her brother
Jim knew more about the origin of our father
than they ever told us.

"Miss Minty," as we children called her,
would think nothing of taking us into her
home and seating us at her table. This was
contrary to the unwritten law of Maryland.

Well, if we are of German origin, this is not
the most auspicious time to look it up, while
the Kaiser is in such disfavor.

When I became old enough to really appreciate the greatness of my mother, who despite
my lowly birth, planned for my future, on
blind faith, I went to the site of the homestead to get a souvenir from one of the logs
of the house in which I was born. A new
house stood on the spot. "Aunt Caroline"
went behind the house in search of a log that

might still remain, but, was doomed to disappointment.

However, that is the spot. The pear tree has long since ceased to exist. The old well, as dear to us as was Jacob's well, to his posterity, is filled up, but a sunken place in the ground, a few paces from what was the northwest corner of the dear old house, tells the story.

My mother always referred to me as her "Christmas gift." I was born between sundown, December 24th and daybreak, December 25th.

We had no clock in the house, and the people in those days did not go to bed at all on "Christmas Eve Night," and it may have been after midnight when I came. But the record in the old family Bible says:

"Levi Jenkins Coppin, born December 24th, 1848." The "Christmas gift" idea is all right, for Santa Claus is always credited with coming at night and not in the morning.

No one can ever know exactly just what a mother is thinking about her children, or why she does this thing or that.

The sentiment that clustered about the time of my birth enabled mother to observe the day with a "birthday dinner" without seeming to

show partiality. Neither did any of the other
children ever show the least dissatisfaction
because the "fatted calf" was killed only once
a year.

I discovered early in life that I was always
the one called up when company came to
"speak a piece," and to tell what day of the
month it was; and later on to get down the
Farmers' Almanac, and tell about the "full
and changes of the moon." Tell about the man
standing there with "Pharaoh's plagues" all
around him, punching him; and to read, to
the admiration of the listening hosts, "con-
jectures of the weather." With an eloquence
that held all spellbound, I would cry out,
"first and second, clear; third and fourth,
cloudy; fifth and sixth, variable; seventh and
eighth, showers, etc."

Grandmother Lilly discovered an aptness
about Jane, that the other children did not
possess, and slipped her off to Baltimore.

Baltimore being in the State of Maryland,
"free Negroes" from other parts of the State
might go and come freely, so long as there
was no suspicion of an ulterior motive.

If such a person was suspected of whisper-
ing to the slaves, or, clandestinely conveying
passes, an accusation was equivalent to con-

viction, and for such a crime the offender could be sold to the highest bidder outside of the State and henceforth made a slave.

It is no wonder that so few would undertake to "run the blockade." Runaway slaves, if captured, were entirely at the mercy of the master. The other slaves were made to form a cordon, while the culprit, in the midst, received such punishment as was thought best to terrify the other slaves.

Sometimes it would be a terrible castigation from the overseer. Sometimes the wife, or husband, or child of the victim would be selected to apply the punishment.

I heard of a case once, where the victim was cut up piece by piece and fed to the bloodhounds. And so it required a great deal of courage for a slave to run away, or, for a "free nigger" to be caught learning to read and write, for he would be accused of preparing to write passes for slaves in the name of their masters.

Amelia Lilly was willing to take so great a risk as this with her most likely child, and so, Jane was sent to Baltimore, ostensibly to live with her aunt, Lucy Harding, but, in fact, it was that her Aunt Lucy might find some one who would teach her to read and write; and so she did.

When mother came home on a visit one time, father, a man of taste and good judgment soon discovered that she was above the mark set by the custom of the place, and so, was bold and daring enough to seek her heart and hand, and not in vain.

What gave him an idea that he was worthy of the foremost young woman in Cecil County, so granted by common consent, no one knows.

Why not be wooed and won by a Baltimore lad, who could boast at least of having "city ways," a thing quite unknown to a "country clodhopper." Well, it is hard to tell just how far presumtiousness will go when once started. It may even be inherited.

Father had a habit of consulting mother on all important matters, and I think, generally took her advice. She was quick to reach a conclusion, and not easily changed from an opinion.

There were two things upon which they did not entirely agree in the earlier days, at least of their married life. First, father could not see the wisdom of taking such risks as mother would take, to teach the children to read and write. Of what service could it ever be to them?

The majority of the children held to the opinion of father, but the "Christmas baby" inclined to side with mother, and this fact made them early companions, much earlier than the average child is called into parental council.

Another point on which father and mother differed somewhat was, father always regarded mother as being recklessly generous.

Every old woman in the neighborhood formed a habit of visiting our home frequently, especially about hog-killing time.

When the winter set in, and the visitors could not make their customary itinerary, we boys knew where they lived, and knew how to go and hunt them up, carrying the practical compliments of mother; and not make known where we had been and for what purpose, a fireside talk upon our return.

Those dear old women would call mother "Cousin Jane." Father would speak derisively of such relationships, and characterized it as "swap dog kin."

I have often heard mother say: "I shall never want for bread," and she did not.

The philosophy of father was different. He thought the best way to keep away want was to kill several fat hogs; bury a plenty of potatoes and cabbages; dry and preserve much fruit; salt away a barrel of herrings and pile up cord after cord of wood at the "wood pile," and his theory was, let others do the same.

My mother did not at all object to such a course, for she was hand in hand with him in providing. But she believed in sharing with others, especially the unfortunate and needy.

I was sent to the store one cold day with orders to go by the little hut where "Aunt Ruthy" lived. This was not even "Swap dog" relation.

The white people did not permit us to say "Mr." and "Mrs." to each other, so, the children, for "manner's sake," were taught to call the older people, "aunt" and "uncle."

Well, I called as I was directed, at the house of "Aunt Ruthy." She was shivering before a few not very live coals, for, the wood must not be burned extravagantly. When I got ready to go, she said, "Leevie, tell your mother, while the grass grows, the steed is starving."

I had never heard of a "steed" before, and thought "Aunt Ruthy" had surely made a mistake. And besides, I could not see how mother would make the application.

So, to help mother out somewhat, I changed the phraseology a little, and said: "Aunt Ruthy says, while the grass grows the sheep are starving."

I knew what a sheep was.

A few minutes later I found myself on the way back to "Aunt Ruthy's with a basket of meat and potatoes, from my father's smoke-house.

That was the interpretation of the starving steed.

In after years, father came to understand mother's philosophy better. When the opportunity unexpectedly came for the children to go to school, mother was not more anxious than father that we should go, and he also learned at last, that, they who sow bountifully, reap also bountifully.

Mother was a Christian as far back as I can remember. The fact is, she embraced religion when a girl.

The children, one by one, so soon as they could pronounce words, said prayers before going to bed, and said "thank the Lord" after each meal.

Father was not a churchman, though I never heard him swear. And not a child up to his manhood was ever allowed to swear before him.

In this particular thing I was always like my father and have my first oath yet to swear. In this, I differed from the other boys.

Father, as well as mother, despised lieing, stealing and drunkenness, and the weight of their influence, both by precept and example, was always in favor of a pure moral atmosphere in the home.

But still, as my father made no profession of religion, and could not lead his household in family worship, it threw the burden of religious duty on mother.

To neglect early religious training is to leave out that which is most important in the formative period of a life. And this is especially true of those, who, by social ostracism, are deprived of coming in contact with uplifting influence outside of the home.

When the father is the patriarch, leading the family in daily devotions, it is not difficult to establish in the home a respect for morals and religion. But when the head of the house is not responsible for such law and order, the mother, in order to bring it about, must be unusually strong in personality, and courage, and faith.

Some of my very earliest recollections are upon moral and religious subjects.

My mother used to take me to church and have me sit in the "Amen corner" with her. I was too young to have any opinion about anything that took place. I remember that after preaching, class meeting would follow, and one after another would get up and speak. Mother would frequently sing between these speeches. She was the one who was really depended upon to sing at the "Meeting house."

She had a clear, ringing voice, which could be detected above the other voices, no matter how large the chorus.

She used to sing:

"John carried his number over."
Moses led the children home.
We'll join the forty thousand, by and by."

And "We Are the True Born Sons of Levi," and many other like songs. Also the good old Methodist hymns, such as:

"Am I a Soldier of the Cross?" "When I Can Read My Title Clear" and "O, Joyful Sound of Gospel Grace," "My God, the Spring of All My Joy." But whether on the make-as-you-go hymns or the standards, mother was quite at home, and was always in great demand.

If the meeting became a little dull, the leader would call out, "Sister Coppin, sing something." No sooner would the words fall from his lips than that familiar voice would ring out, and soon things would be going at a lively pace.

The old church leaders, as a rule, did not know many hymns by heart. They used to call them "hymes." My mother had this advantage of them, she could read, and would learn hymn after hymn, and sing them from memory.

There was a Bible and hymn book in our home ever since I can remember any thing.

Once, when mother took me to church—I must have been very small—I remember there was a little fat yellow woman who got very happy while singing a piece. The fact is, some of them would apparently get quite happy after the first or second verse, if that was all they knew; then some one else would have to catch it up and go on with it, if it went any further. This was one of "Uncle" Abe Kennard's tricks.

But, on this particular occasion, the singer was "Aunt" Fanny Bayard. There were two peculiarities about the song that so impressed me, that I still remember them vividly, namely:

First, she sang so fast that no one could catch on and accompany her. ·Secondly, in her "Hallelujah" she repeated the "Halle, and would say:

"We've found the rock, the traveler cried,
  Glory halle, hallelujah."

As I remember now, she made only one double or single line and chorous, and that with such rapidity that no one got hold of the words or rhyme; then suddenly she exclaimed, "Glory to God, Glory to God!" and all was over.

She was short and fat, and had what people called, "poppy eyes." I never did lose sight of her; and when I grew older, I came to know her well. She was a free woman, a widow with one daughter, Henrietta—"Henny" she called her—and lived in her own little house at Crooktown, near Cecilton.

Crooktown and Perrytown were two little clusters of houses—huts—that were behind the woods that separated Cecilton from where the free colored people lived.

There were not many families in these little settlements, but the woods, i. e., the grove, spoken of in another chapter, afforded a meeting place for our people, bond and free.

After I visited South Africa, and saw some of the original Hottentots, I was led to believe that "Aunt" Fanny Bayard was one of them.

The Hottentot is exactly the color of the Chinese; so was "Aunt" Fanny. They have little tufts of hair scattered about on their heads. I do not know what was on "Aunt" Fanny's head, except that kerchief, that I never saw her without.

The Hottentot is said to live to a very old age. Well, "Aunt" Fanny and her daughter "Henny" lived to be very old. They were companions, and were nearly always together. The boys used to say that "Henny lived until she caught up with her mother."

Henny got married late in life. I do not know whether this was her first husband or not, but one thing I do know, that she outlived him; but "Aunt" Fanny outlived her.

When the little old hut was about to fall down on her, she made over the place to "Father Jones," and he built a little frame house on it, in which "Aunt" Fanny ended her days.

Besides "Aunt" Fanny; Emory Sisco, John Hall and Benjamin Freeman lived in Crooktown. All of them free people.

Living at Perrytown, which was but a few hundred yards from Crooktown, was a man named Perry Thompson. He was said to be a very wicked man.

A man thus characterized by our people was one who would swear, drink whisky and perhaps gamble; one who never went to church. They were called hard-hearted sinners.

Some of them were supposed to have "dealings" with the Devil. When such a person died, you could not get a neighborhood child to go any distance alone at night.

The impression was, the devil had come for the wicked person, and was probably still sneaking about there in the darkness.

This doctrine was quite generally believed by the older ones, and the children had no inclination to go out into the darkness and investigate it, in order to be convinced whether it was true or false.

There was always a superstition that the death of such a person was accompanied by a storm, a terrible storm, preferably a snow storm.

By some kind of coincidence, the biggest snow storm of the season often came at the time of the death of such persons.

I remember the Perry Thompson snow storm. What a time they had getting him buried! These wicked people would often die swearing and raving, crying, "drive out them dogs."

Of course, the modern physician can easily account for his delirious condition. But, even now, I have a lingering thought, that this doctrine of demoniacal visitation was so prevalent that some of those old sinners felt doomed, and just became mentally unbalanced in expectation of meeting their just deserts.

In those days, you would often hear hymns like this:

"And must I be to judgement brought,
    To answer in that day
For every vain and idle thought,
    And every word I say?"

"Yes, every secret of my heart,
    Shall surely be made known;
And I'll receive my just deserts,
    Fo all that I have done."

German "higher criticism" was not much heard of then, neither was a world war!

I do not claim to believe the many superstitions that I heard in my childhood, but I am glad that certain impressions were made upon me then, instead of some others that might have been made.

I was well up in my teens before I found out that the devil did not come with a pitchfork after boys who would lie and steal, and swear and get drunk. But I was so long in finding out that he did not come and literally catch them, that, having formed the habit of shunning these forbidden things, I just considered that there were other good reasons why these practices should be avoided, and so went on avoiding them.

When I was a child, they told me about "Kris Kringle," the country folks called him. I believed, with all my young, innocent heart, that such a person existed.

Finally some "smarty" told me that there was no such person, and "let the cat out of the bag."

But that is only half of the truth. The fact is that I am still afraid of the devil, whatever may be the reason for my fear.

But since I have become grown, I have found that there is a Santa who fills the heart with love and sympathy, and especially, about the "Christmas season."

No one shall ever again be able to convince me that no such spirit exists.

Many other impressions made in boyhood, thanks to the simple faith of a pious mother, have saved me from the dashing currents of sin, by which I have seen others swept away.

The history of the mothers of this period can never be known. The story of the Exodus from Egypt begins with the birth of Moses, and the mother who hid him until she could no longer do so with safety.

Then the story of the basket of rushes, by which the babe of providence was floated on the water until found by the princess.

Then the mother nurse, according to the mother plan. When it was time to hand him over to the adopted mother at the royal court, his own mother had made such lasting impressions upon him, that they proved stronger than the very strong temptation to "enjoy the pleasures of sin for a season."

The writer of the Pentateuch gives us this story of a mother's love and wisdom and successful training.

In both religious and secular history, we have the maternal part played in the world's history, until it is accepted as true that "the hand that rocks the cradle rules the world."

The story of the mother of Moses is the oldest of such stories, and the scene was in Egypt, and Egypt is in Africa.

But the bond woman brought from Africa had no one to write of her wisdom and heroism. Some things would be passed down by tradition from generation to generation and then be forgotten.

With the unwritten history of the race is buried most of the best things that are really characteristic of the race originally.

Two hundred and fifty years developed a new people, with new traditions, customs, morals and religion, copied from the dominant people of their new environment.

But whether written or unwritten, the history of the African in America from 1619 to 1865, constitutes a most interesting chapter in the book of human events.

CHAPTER II.

Social, Moral and Intellectual Conditions

Maryland—my Maryalnd—is the northern-most Southern State. Its northern boundary is the famous Mason and Dixon's Line.

On account of its geographical location it is often erroneously referred to as a Northern State. But, not only did the earlier geographies class it as Southern, but it stood pat as such when it became the fashion to sub-divide the sections; as, for instance: "West and Middle West." Maryland never was classified with Delaware as a "Middle State." Mason and Dixon settled the question once and for all, and the Marylanders, bond and free, have never tried to blot out the line, nor to claim to have been born "further up."

Being a Southern State, Maryland was a Slave State. The institution prospered there, as it did in Georgia, though no cotton was grown there.

(32)

It may not be generally known that Maryland laws and customs were more oppressive to the slave and "Free Negro" than were the laws and customs of States farther south.

For instance, Negroes in South Carolina have owned slaves; such a thing would never have been, and according to slave code philosophy—could never have been permitted in Maryland. Upper Maryland is on the line of Pennsylvania, the Quaker State; the hot-bed of abolition; the first state to protest mildly, then vigorously, against slavery, and then to deal it a death blow by becoming the headquarters and principal station of the Underground Railroad, and furnishing the principal officers of the line. When a few thousand were once offered for the head of "Thomie" Garrett, he said: "Five hundred slaves have passed through my hands, and never a one was captured." He was a Pennsylvania Quaker, conducting a sub-underground station in Wilmington, Del. The big barns of the Tatnals, just across the Bandywine, were often filled with fugitives, many of whom were of Thomie Garrett's "five hundred."

The relation of Maryland, then, to free soil, and to the abolition propaganda, made it necessary for the slave owner, and the slave trader to keep a sharp watch on the border, and to keep the lines taut on the slave and the "free nigger." Each must know his place and never forget it, and each must be kept in mortal fear of the master, the trader, and the spy. A free Negro might not go out of the state and return under the penalty of being fined a sum that he would not be expected to be able to pay without the assistance of the Georgia trader, or the more humane (?) gentleman who would pay the fine, and give the victim a chance to work it out upon such terms as the benefactor dictated.

Being so close to the line, a Maryland slave had to be constantly and closely watched lest he "run away." The farther one was removed from the North Star the more difficult it was to use it as a guide to freedom. The Underground Railroad could not operate freely in the far South, and so, the slaves stood a far better chance of being "Trusties."

Some of the border line slave owners established a custom of whipping the slaves once a week, "every Monday morning," to keep them humble and in fear. Early in the morning, while the "Day Spring" stood as a silent witness, against the day when the cup of iniquity would be full, the cry of the slave would break the silence. "O massy, pray massy!" while the lash of the slave driver played its nimble game upon his bare-back. Sometimes to make humility and degra-gradation reach their lowest possible depths, and to destroy the last vestige of personal rights, the slave husband would be made to "cow-hide" the slave wife.

When, in spite of all the vigilance and cruel-ty that could be practiced, there were still some who were characterized as impudent, unruly or, likely to make their escape at some time, and therefore were dangerous to be among other slaves, they would be roped and sold to "Georgia traders." Not that all the traders were from Georgia, nor used that state exclusively as a market, but, the ex-pression "Georgia Trader" became so common that many slaves, and ignorant whites did not know, or think of any other market. An ig-norant mistress would indulge in the threat: "I'll make your master slash your back and sell you to Georgia."

Nothing in these "unwritten pages" is in-tended to revive a feeling of hatred. We stand so far from the scenes herein described that no one is left to be hated and no one is left to hate. Both master and slave have long

since passed away, and the generations then
unborn are now upon the stage of action, with
but a few connecting links. The real object
is to show that even from this Egypt, came a
Moses, a Joshua, A Miriam, of sable hue.
Even from this Nazareth came some good
thing.

We can not even now appreciate the ster·
ling virtue of our women, especially of the
past, until we have been cited to the fact,
that even in these times, not fully here described, only hinted at, when a woman as well
as a man was her master's property just as
was his horse and his dog, there were women,
black women, slave women, who would stand
up and fight the master to the death, and
die virtuous. Or, if considered too valuable
either to kill or to sell, would live to stand
as examples of chastity such as the world
never had seen, and to transmit their spirit
and blood to posterity. The better knowledge
a race has of its own virtues, the less likely
it is to run away from itself, and the more determined it may become to strive for an honorable future.

When freedom at last came, I had a strong
desire to go to Georgia, and see some of the
stock that I had been told went from Mary-

land. My desire was fully gratified in after years; for my good friend, Bishop Gaines, bade me welcome to his Conferences, year after year, as I traveled as a General Officer in the Church. And the men and women of Georgia, whether from Maryland or elsewhere, impressed me that they were of noble origin.

A subject people, especially where slavery dominates, are so far removed from the ruling classes, that socially, they have nothing in common. The contact is as master and slave; as superior and inferior.

In cases where the housemaid was daily with the members of the family and the guests who mingled with them, a difference could be seen in appearance and general deportment. Often the house girl at the Big House was the Lady at the Quarters. She wore the cast-off clothing of her mistress. In many cases, where the mistress was kindly disposed, she took especial pride in dressing her maid in such finery as to place her above the common lot; or, to make her outshine all the neighborhood house girls.

You could tell the girls of "Miss Mary Cruikshanks." She had but one slave woman, Delia: her house girls were hired.

After she established a reputation for bestowing so much thought and care upon her house girls, the mothers of free girls would seek to place their daughters in her household. I think now of two who came up under her care, Rebecca ————, and Julia ————

Being house girls these favored ones would pick up words and expressions that they would use in conversation, and therefore would be considered "smart" by the rank and file.

"Miss Mary" also guarded the morals of her girls, and it was especially for that reason that free women sought to bring their girls under her influence and control, even if they had to "bind them out" to her for a term of years, to make it worth while for her to take them.

But, "Miss Mary Cruikshank" was an exception to the rule. She lived in the village, Her husband was the leading cross roads store-keeper, and sold goods to colored as well as to white. He was a slave holder, but with only four slaves; "Uncle" Jim, Wes (Wesley), Theodore and "Aunt" Deley.

The Cruikshanks were not the old slave-driving class. "Uncle" Jim and "Aunt" Deley were kept with the family in town, while Theodore and Wes were hired out to this and that neighborhood farmer. But the point in question is this: the colored were separated definitely and universally from the whites socially, and hence, permitted to live by such moral codes as originated at the quarters where the wheat and the tares grew together. To be more definite, the colored people were socially placed amid environments where there were no moral codes or restrictions.

Hatched out in the same nests, brought up in a common brood, living and sleeping in the same single room huts—quarters—boys and girls alike grew up together about as the cattle did, with no moral guide or restraint except that which was given by nature.

It was to the interest of the masters that their women servants became mothers. The more frequently, the better, as it multiplied their slaves, and hence their wealth.

A boy who could boast of being a father while still in his teens, was considered worthy of a prize. The girl who was the mother of several children while yet unmarried, and that by different fathers, did not have to carry a "shame face."

While such cases were numerous but one may be cited. A man named James ————, who lived in the Cruikshank village had one slave woman. She became the mother of four boys, with "sir names," respectively: Henson, Harding, Rice and Wilson. The first three grew to manhood and were rented out by the master, before the Civil War. The youngest of the three named entered the war in '63, while the fourth, a lad, with his older brothers, was set free by Lincoln's proclamation. The multiplication of slaves by illegitimate births was not left entirely to the slave men, but the masters and young masters supplemented their lack. But, whether by the blacks or the whites, the birth rate must be kept up.

A man who passed through slavery and finished his years as a member of one of our churches in Philadelphia, relates a story about how he was selected by his master on account of being strong and healthy; relieved of the laborious work of the plantation, and named as the person to be the common law husband (?) of all the women on the place. If any refused to submit they were to be reported to their masters, who with a cat-of-nine tails would teach them how to obey any order that came down from him.

Some masters were "mean and stingy" and did not give their slaves enough to eat, but would indirectly encourage them to steal from neighboring farmers. By "indirectly encouraging them," I mean they were never chastised for doing so. They had but to observe two rules: First, never steal from their master, and second, never get caught.

What a comment on the present day criticism that brands the Negro as being dishonest as to the personal property of others, derelict as to his "promise to pay," and woefully wanting in his regard for sexual purity.

The nameless crime; the crime that cannot be ascribed even to most of the lower animals, who mate, and fellowship only in season, is a crime unknown to the African before being brought into contact with that brand of civilization that is responsible for the World War. A crime unknown to the descendants of Africa before James ———— was told to report to his master any who refused. The crime that filled our land with mulattoes, nolens volens. The crime that so degraded the "proud Anglo-Saxon" that he would sell his own flesh and blood when he became financially embarrassed. The crime for which any man deserves to die: according to the law, of course.

We do not always stop to think that slavery degraded the master even more than the slave. "If ye were blind ye should have no sin: but now ye say, we see; therefore your sin re-maineth." The conditions that were neces-sary to perpetuate slavery, blinded, degraded, and enslaved the masters. Just think of min-isters of Jesus Christ owning, and working and selling slaves.

In our neighborhood there was an Episcopal church on a manor. In the course of time a rector came who brought with him a young woman and a young man, brother and sister. "Jim" and "Hettie" were the only names I ever heard for them. When we wanted to distinguish them from others by the same mono-syllabic names, we would say' "Church Jim and his Sister Hettie." Howbeit, the slave was not allowed to say "sister and brother" in the presence of the master. I came near getting a flogging once because I said to the country storekeeper that I came for a package which "my sister had left there." "Your sis-ter!" he shouted. "Do you mean Mary?" And yet that same man would not hesitate to say that the colt he offered for sale, was sister to the one hitched at the post.

Church Jim and Hettie worked on the church farm; associated with the Negroes of the neighborhood and country. Were no bet-ter and no worse. Jim, just like the rest, might be indulging in a game of cards, or crap while the master preached to the farmers whose horses were hitched about the church-yard.   It was all the same to this civilized Christian (?) parson, just so Hettie had dinner ready after church, and Jim was promptly on hand Monday morning. All the colored people of our Neck—Sasafras—were Methodists.   At that time, in the sixties, I think there was not a Baptist church in that part of the country. There were but few white people who were anything but Methodists.

The "brick church" near the village had a gallery that opened from the outside, with nearly perpendicular steps leading to it. There the colored people went for their spiritual food.   I remember hearing "Uncle Jake Trusty" tell my mother what the minister preached about, and how beautifully he presented the subject. I can now see my mother go to the family Bible, find the text and mark it.   After "Uncle" Jake had satisfied his full-grown appetite and bade "Sister Jane" goodby, my mother would take up the Bible—the old family Bible, where our births are recorded—find the marked place, and have a spell of reading.   "My word shall not return void." My mother and "Uncle" Jake accepted the word even though it came from a Christian (?) minister who denied the brotherhood.

The only other place for them to go and give vent to their religious faith and feelings was "Friendship," a little log house used for a church, indeed, built for that purpose. "Uncle" Perry Hinson, a free Negro, owned an acre or two of ground behind the woods that was near to Cecilton. On it he built a few one-room cabins, and this church. All built of logs.

This little settlement, with "Friendship," became the social and religious centre of the people five and ten miles around, and "Uncle" Perry Hinson, the proprietor, became the all important man of the place. He could read a little bit in a blundering way, when he could get his "specks" properly adjusted; and claimed the right to preach. He had built the church on his own ground, and it was no part of the Cecilton Circuit of the Methodist Episcopal Church. Had no trustees nor stewards. No quarterly conference to grant license or refuse to renew them. And so, "Uncle" Perry saw no reason why he might not exercise his gifts and graces on the colored folk who came to "Friendship" to worship.

For a long time he had things his own way. Free people and slaves alike would gather to "Perry Town," as the place came to be called. The grove of oak trees in front was the most magnificent natural grove I ever saw. The crowds would gather there, especially in summer. There was no other such gathering place in the county, though Cecil county is large.

The white people would come around oc-occasionally to see that all went well, and no mischief was being hatched out at those meetings. The fact is, they were glad for the people to have such a place to meet and satisfy their social and spiritual nature, and foster the spirit of contentment among themselves rather than to discover their true condition and brood over it.

The grove immediately in front of Friendship contained about thirty acres of ground, all wooded, and all trees of large growth, principally oaks. I think it is safe to say there was not in all of that beautiful grove a single sapling that might have been used as a "pea stick." Strange to say, it was never resorted to by the people of the town, as a park, or, excursion grounds; nor did the owner cut any of the trees, nor permit others to cut them. By common consent it was left standing and undistrubed for the colored people to use as their gathering place. Not until after freedom was the woodman's axe heard in this grove ; and then (the whole story seems prophetic) enough of it was left, about an acre, for a school house for colored children. This school is kept open during the same school period of all other schools of the county.

"Uncle" Perry Hinson, as I have said, held undisputed sway as self-appointed pastor in charge of Friendship until others discovered that they had a "talent," and at the same time discovered that the pulpit was the only open door of opportunity for its exercise and improvement. These came forward one after another in a sort of automatic way, the same as "Uncle" Perry had come.

From time to time these new "speakers," as they were called, would be asked to take the pulpit. Uncle Perry tolerated it for a time, but, when the invitations became too frequent for his liking he locked the church door, and upon being questioned as to his action, he would ask the significant question: "Who is the head of this church." Well, it was found to be wise and prudent to humor "Unc." Perry by allowing him to do the most of the preaching, and thus keep the peace, and at the same time keep Friendship open.

But what of the intellectual status of the people during those days of slavery and primitive life?

"Unto one he gave five talents, to another two, to another one."

Whatever was nature's endowment it remained in a natural state, with no opportunity for improvement. School-houses were built for white people. School-books were written for white children. After years, even centuries of practical demonstration, all the colored people came to know that fact by heart, and so, did not concern themselves about school-houses, books, or learning. If those talents, the endowment of nature, began to whisper in their souls, they could give vent to the emotions by inventing riddles, and practicing fortune telling, and "conjuration."

Many would exercise this pent-up gift by discussing self-made philosophy among themselves. At this some were considered "very smart." They called it "high dictionary" and those who were most expert in it, could generally capture the girls who were considered the belles, for some of them, as well as the men, could talk "high dictionary" and explain "hifullutin grammar."

When this natural gift took a mechanical bent, the pocket-knife would be brought into requisition to make some kind of ornament; or, it might even take a more scientific turn.

Jack Price—who, by the way is still living, and is a Grand Army Veteran—took his watch to pieces, cleaned it and put it up again, using no other tools than his fingers. I am not sure that it ever ran any more. But the next one who tried it, namely Josh Ferrell, made a success of it, and opened a clock and watch repairing shop in Cecilton, and did work for the people of the town. He was a free Negro.

Those who had musical talent often became "fiddlers," and some of them were considered quite expert with the bow. Of course, they knew nothing about the science of music. They played the jingles for the buck dances at corn huskings, parties and the holiday gatherings, of which "Easter Monday" was the principal.

It never occurred to the colored people in general that Easter was a religious holiday. With them, Easter was simply a day, when by common consent of all the masters, the blacks had holiday. Not a "Holy day," but a day when they could rest from the routine toil, and select their own pastime. With them, Easter was Monday, without any connection whatever with Sunday. If the story of the Resurrection was told at all, it was at the churches which the slave did not attend. Even the "house girls" did not go to white folks' church usually. At certain seasons there would be "protracted meetings," sometimes called revival meetings. They would continue indefinitely, according to the interest awakened. At these meetings the colored people would be allowed to sit in the gallery and see the whites "get religion."

They would get at it in good old Methodist style; at least, so far as the mourner's bench was concerned.

The singing would be of the revival type. One of the favorites for such occasions was, the familiar hymn:

"Come Ye sinners, poor, and needy,
Weak and wounded, sick and sore.
Jesus ready stands to save you
Full of pity, love and power." With the chorus:

"Turn to the Lord and seek salvation,
Sound the praise of His dear name.
Glory, honor, and salvation,
Christ the Lord has come to reign."

They also had "made up" hymns for the
occasion; such as:

We're happy here in the clods of clay.
    Cho. Glory hallelujah!
And happy in an endless day.
    Glory hallelujah!

Brother Sylvester Stephens, a big fat man,
carpenter by trade, was the leading singer at
the "brick church." He sat on the seat next
to the wall, front row, in the "amen corner."
There was no choir. Brother Stephens would
pitch all the tunes, and on revival occasions
be very active among the mourners. He had
the reputation of saying he did not want to
go to heaven if any "niggers" were there. I
cannot vouch for this; but like many ignorant men of his type, he was mean toward the
colored man. Being both ignorant and poor,
he could only base his superiority upon his
color. Not that the colored man had ever done
him any harm; but to despise him, was considered the way to show that he, Stephens,

was genuinely white. His house caught on fire one day, and burned to the ground. It is now fresh in my mind. It was one afternoon. Many of us saw the flames, and heard the cracking of the fire as it swept away the dry timber. I do not think that many of the colored people went into sackcloth and ashes over the loss, tho, for policy sake, many expressed sorrow and sympathy. Prejudice is an awful thing. It is more far reaching in its effects than we are wont to give it the credit of being. The man who indulges the feeling, is fostering a bitterness of soul that is like a hissing serpent in the bosom. The one who is the victim of it, may have a feeling of vindictiveness that keeps him so constantly on the alert that often innocent persons are accused. Color prejudice, of all kinds, seems the most shallow and unreasonable. Might as well be prejudiced to black berries, and "black heart" cherries: or to black cats, and black horses: or black clothing, or anything black.

Perhaps it is not the color after all. The color identifies one with a "previous condition." Clandestine fellowship was not objectionable. For this, there is abundant proof. Men will dispise those whom they can degrade. The

color of the Negro identifies him with those
whom the white man enslaved and degraded.

It is but fair and just to note, that even in
the darkest days of slavery, there were those
who were among the seven thousand who
never bowed to Baal, nor kissed his image.
Among them were some ministers who pastored at the "brick church."

On one occasion there came a minister who
was at heart an abolitionist, and would at
times preach against the sin of slave holding.
It was a minister of this class who in the
hearing of the Master of Richard Allen, preach
ed from the text: "Thou art weighed in the
balance and art found wanting." Among those
whom he weighed, was the slave holder. The
Master was so condemned, that he offered to
allow Richard to purchase his freedom; which
he did.

So, the minister referred to, preached one
Sunday morning against slavery. It is said
that he was very severe in his arraignment
of the master class.

When he was thru, the services were
changed as usual into the Sunday morning
Class Meeting. There was a sister, a slave
holder, who generally led off by giving her experience before Brother Stephens began to

lead. So, tho smarting under the sting of the sermon, she arose, and began to speak, but not with her usual clearness. Her voice trembled, and she stammeringly felt about for words. The minister who was responsible for her state of mind, discovering her embarrassment, shouted out: "spit them niggers out of your throat, sister."

The colored people in the gallery had news to take away with them that morning. Many of them would remain in their little secluded lofts until after "class." They were glad that some remained on this occasion, for what followed, strengthened them in their faith, that God was not without witnesses, and that some day, in His own way, at His own time, deliverance would come. It was this faith and this hope that sustained our fathers and mothers during the long period of darkness and oppression, and its transmission to posterity was a legacy more valuable than the heaped up riches which they earned, but did not possess.

The colored people were encouraged to "get religion." It was thought that it would make them more contented. They would learn to sing: "You May Have All The World, Give Me Jesus." This song when properly interpreted, simply means, if one is obilged to make a choice between Jesus and the world, it would pay to take Jesus. But all were not intelligent enough to draw such sharp lines of distinction. And besides, they were taught to believe that the poor and oppressed stood a better chance for Heaven than the rich, and such as have a good time in this world. When we would see people riding in fine carriages, we would say: "that is all the heaven you will ever get." When the slave trader would buy up a lot, and start on a certain day to the place of embarkation, they would sing as they marched: "you may sell my body, but you cannot sell my soul." They were not taught that they had need to be careful about living righteously. This would have been against the indiscriminate living that produced slaves with the desired rapidity. The code of moral given to the slaves, was, weak human nature could not help sinning, but it was only necessary to ask for forgiveness. In this way two things could be accomplished; the slave could be made religious, and yet kept debased.

Christianity gave the slave holders a good deal of trouble, but they some how managed to get on, with a compromise. The question of baptism and marriage came up for discussion. Was not a baptised person a child of God and hence free? Did not the wife belong to the husband? how then could she have another owner? All this was logically and Biblically true enough, but, the compromise was, it did not necessarily follow that slaves must be either baptised or married.

One of the big days among our people was, when a funeral was held.

A person from New Jersey who was not acquainted with our customs, heard it announced that: "next Sunday two weeks the funeral of Jenet Anderson will be preached. "Well" said the stranger, "how do they know that she will be dead." The fact was, she was already dead, and had been for some time. But, according to our custom, a custom growing out of necessity, we did not hold the funeral when the person was buried. The relatives —and friends—could not leave their work to attend funerals. Often persons would be buried at night after working hours. If the deceased was a free person, and the immediate family could attend a week day funeral, there might be others, both friends and relatives who could not attend, hence, the custom became general.

When the day was fixed upon the news would be sent "far and near;" and on the day, if weather conditions were favorable, there would be: "a meeting here today."

The usual place was old "Friendship" yes dear old Friendship behind the big woods. For miles and miles around they would come: Aunts, uncles, cousins, friends, and the curious ones; and all who would sieze the opportunity to meet friends and relatives. The mourners would be heavily clad in black, even if only dark colored calico. The men would have heavy black bands around their hats. All would occupy the front seats. Nothing strange would be thought of the absence of coffin and subject. All knew that he had not only been dead for "four days," but, four months, or years for that matter. "Father Jones" would be selected to preach the funeral whenever his services could be secured. Strange enough too, he had the reputation of "telling the truth' about the persons funeralized, and not preaching them "into heaven" whether or not. If it were a wife whose husband had been unkind to her, Father Jones would say: "poor woman! She is done being cuffed around and starved." The scandalized husband would be sitting right there among the mourners. But, by common consent, as it were, Father Jones was expected to preach in this way, and would still be chosen by others. He was without a doubt, a famous preacher, and came so honestly, for he was remarkably talented. People who never attended church, would go if it was known that he would preach. He read his Bible constantly and was familiar with its contents. He was fond of Old Testament subjects, especially historic subjects, and his narrations were most interesting, and his applications most forceful. He was a man of untarnished character, and lived above suspicion, hence, it was considered an honor to have him officiate at a funeral, or on any occasion.

Very often, the masters of favorite slaves would have their funerals preached at the "big house." On such occasions, Father Jones would always be selected. The gathering would be on and in front of the Veranda. The white people would be guests of honor. The colored people would occupy seats placed on the lawn in front of the Veranda. Father Jones would line out a long hymn, verse by verse: such as: "Hark! From the Tomb a Doleful sound, my ears attend the cry.

Ye living men, come view the ground
Where you must shortly lie."

This would be pitched in a minor tune—
the most of our tunes were minors—La, la,
sol, do: Sol la, la, me.

Do, me, re, do, sol, do. This would be sung
with much feeling, as the body would be
swayed back and forth. After prayer, would
follow the sermon. And such a sermon! The
preacher knew where he was, and exactly
what to do.

Generally, of course, the servant thus honored was in high repute, and also, had been
treated well, and Father Jones knew just how
to praise the masters and mistresses who had
been so kind to their slaves. A big dinner for
all and a five dollar bill for the preacher would
end the service.

Before the close of the war, the colored
people would be permitted to hold meetings
in their church—Friendship—but the white
people kept a close watch as a rule. Some one
would drop around frequently, and they were
obliged to have a white class leader who would
be selected and sent to them. James Magee
a butcher was one, I am told. The only one
that I remember was John Russel a shoe

maker. Both claimed to be flaming Method-ists.

According to the custom of the times they were not expected to use the good old appel-lation brother and sister. What a travesty on both Methodism and Christianity!

"John, tell us how your soul prospers." "Betsy, tell the class."

A leader of this kind once asked the one who had just finished his testimony, if he had stolen any chickens from his master since he last led him. Of course, the reply was in the negative. But when the leader passed on to the next person, the one who had been in-terrogated, nudged the one next to him, and remarked: "if he had said 'duck' he would have got me."

Then as now, there were the "sheep" and the "goats," as the Bible designates. There were those, whose moral shortcomings were without excuse. But, there were also some who, like John the Baptist, were "burning and shining lights." Real, "salt of the Earth." Their conversion was sound, and their lives were pure. They were spiritually wise, how-ever ignorant as to the things of earth. They knew God, and held with Him sweet Com-

munion.   They could rejoice in tribulation,
and let their light shine in the humblest walks
of life.

In prayer and in exhortation they had remarkable freedom of speech, and power with
God.   The influence of their lives was felt in
the Quarter and at the great house.   They
were trusted, not to say respected, both by
master and fellow slaves.   The world   was
not worthy of them; and they died in the
faith and were translated to the Saints' abode,
where the "Lamb upon the throne" shall "wipe
away all tears from their eyes."

There swooped down upon us once, a man,
who came as suddenly as did Elijah the Tish-
bite.   His name was Samuel Black.   He came
from Kent County.   He was one of those self
licensed   local preachers, of   whom we   had
quite a number, before there was any one to
give license.   He   was not   remarkably intelligent like Father Jones.   He couldn't take
a passage of scripture and instruct his hear-
ers like the old sage of Back Street, but he
was very remarkable in other respects, and
in a class to himself.

When he felt that he was called of God to
exhort his people, and to be a religious leader among them, he could not read, and saw

no opportunity to get instructions. Besides, he was already a grown man, and with a mind showing no special aptness for taking in book learning. He nevertheless, like many others, began to pray, and exhort, and hold meetings; but, felt the need of being able to read. So he asked God to teach him, and let that be an evidence of his call to preach. He states that one day he took his little hymn book and began to read hymns. Being encouraged by this, he opened his Bible, and began to read from it.

The people had so much confidence in his integrity, that no one doubted his story. He used to prophesy that he would live to this and that period: "until the budding of the trees," or, "until the falling of the leaves." At the stated period he would reappear and remind us that God had kept His promise. He would also ask God for souls when going out on preaching itineraries, and would tell the number that he was promised. His preaching was of the Evangelistic kind: thought nothing of doctrinal discussion, and knew nothing of rhetorical elegance, or, grammatical correctness. But he cried "repent" and lifted up Christ as the World's Redeemer, and warned sinners of the wrath to come. He went out from among us as suddenly as he came. Simply did not come back any more. I met a man in Philadelphia from Kent Co. named Black. When I asked him if he knew the Rev. Samuel Black, he replied: "he was my father." The resemblance was pronounced.

CHAPTER III.

The Civil War.

"Coming events cast their shadows before them."

The decade between 1855 and 1865 brought about marvelous changes.

In the earlier part of this decade, the agitation over the extension of slavery, and its abolition, reached a most acute stage.

The Presidential election of 1856, was the last under the old regime: the last of its kind forever.

The campaigns and discussions that filled the period '56, to '60, were characteristic of the spirit and determination of pro slavery to continue, extend, and strengthen the system; and of a like spirit on the part of the anti slavery advocates, to bring it to an end.

In those days, men spoke pro and con with no uncertain voice. The press was filled with discussions, and every fireside was vocal with opinion for and against State rights, the preservation of the Union, and the abolition of slavery.

These were the days when the house girl and the carriage driver picked up a plenty of news to carry down to the Quarters. These were the days when the faithful ones at the Quarters discovered a ray of the light of hope, and prayed more earnestly that the day would dawn soon. Like Simeon, some of them felt assured that God would show them His salvation, before they were called to cross the narrow stream.

Uncle Jacob Trusty: Uncle Perry Crawford: Uncle Perry Naudain and the veritable old Prophet among them, "Father" Christopher Jones, took their Bibles to find passages that would throw light upon the subject.

The intelligence of these men, and many others was most remarkable. Just how some of them learned to read, will ever remain a mystery.

Chief among these Bible readers, and the peacher, was Father Jones. He was regarded as the moral and intellectual light of the County. Everybody "white and black" believed in his integrity, and relied upon his word with a sort of superstitious fidelity. He was sought by representative men of the place. Men who represented its wealth and culture would solicit his opinion upon the leading topics of the day.

It is fair to conclude that many of them did not know that he could read. They called him "smart" and believed that he lived close to God. And the more they felt that a political crisis was impending, the more anxious they were to know what "Old Kit Jones" thought about it.

There was a school teacher in Cecilton, Samuel Hays by name. He was an abolishionist, but, like Nicodemus, he did not speak out boldly. But he and Father Jones would meet "by night" and go over the situation. But more, Mr. Hays subscribed to a newspaper in his own name, but it was paid for by Father Jones, and secretly passed to him. This went on for years; and during the period immediately preceeding the war, and also while it was in progress, Father Jones had first hand news which he gave out cautiously, from time to time, to his people.

He was not so much for resorting to the prophecies of Daniel for information, as he was to the newspaper that secretly came weekly to him, tho he did not discourage those who did.

He was a very conspicuous looking man. Six feet and five inches high. "Chestnut sorrel" complexion. His features were delicately formed and pronounced. His piercing eye could read character at a glance. He was of the "still tongue and wise head" class.

He worked by contract. For instance, instead of cradling wheat by the day—there were no reapers then—he would take a fifty or hundred acre field by contract. He and his binder would go out early in the morning and work 'till late at night, cut, bind, and shock the field in a few days. He would pull blades and cut cord wood in the same way. Would pay so much an acre for the privilege of pulling the blades, then sell the fodder. Would pay so much for a tract of standing wood, cut it down and sell it by the cord. The black and white oak principally. Hickory would be selected and corded to itself, and sold for more per cord than the oak. No coal was burned in our neighborhood then. There were large tracts of woodland every where. Giant oaks filled the forests. The farmers were too busy to cut more wood than they needed for home consumption, and so,

Christopher Jones developed an industry all his own. The people came to expect him to have wood to sell all winter, and he had. He knew how to make a bargain and he knew how to stand before a white man with his hat in his hand, and with a smile and good words so charm him, that the contract when made would mean money for Jones.

By his method of work, a method all his own, he made a small fortune while he was young and strong, and retired from work before he was broken down, and lived at ease in "Back Street," which consisted of a cluster of five houses which he built on a small tract of land about a quarter of a mile on the North side of Cecilton. Crooktown and Perrytown were on the South side and behind the woods. "Back Street" was adjacent property owned by "Bob" Price, who married Miss Araminta Coppin. As I see it now, Christopher Jones had a reason for selecting that particular spot. It was close to town, but not on the front pike, and besides, being adjacent the Price property, it enjoyed a certain kind of protection. Christopher Jones married my father's mother, a widow. He was therefore, Dad's step father. We all called him "Father Jones." One more child was born to Grand mother

Coppin-Jones, a daughter. She married a Philadelphian, and was a member of Central Presbyterian Church. It was first called Glaucester Church as he was the founder and first pastor.

After his wife died, Father Jones lived quietly in Back Street in the central, and largest house of the group, and father and mother sold out their claim on the Frederick Town homestead to my father's only sister, and moved to Back Street, and lived with Father Jones. I was two small to remember when we moved. My first recollections are of Back Street, and Cecilton.

The talk of war, so absorbed the thought of the people, and controlled public sentiment, that the colored people were no longer the sole objects of attention. The fact is, no one was buying slaves, for it began to look like they would be set free. This put the "Georgia Trader" out of business. The slaves were not watched so closely. Some masters boldly said if their slaves ran away, they would not try to find them.

Under the influence of this changed sentiment quite a number made their escape, some going no farther than Pennsylvania, but even more going to New Jersey. But many concluded to "stand still and see the salvation of God." Father Jones gave this advice in general, tho, there were cases when even he would say, "make your escape by all means." There were masters who would be mean enough to put a slave to death rather than to see him set free through the changed political conditions of the country. But, these were exceptional cases. The fact is, great fear came upon the people. They felt that their sins were about to find them out. They were something like the Canaanites when the Armies of Israel crossed Jordan. "The hearts of the people melted within them."

The election of Abraham Lincoln in the fall of 1860, was the beginning of the end. Events came then in rapid succession.

Maryland was never a battlefield, but Virginia and Pennsylvania were, and we could hear the booming of cannon.

The changed sentiment at the beginning of the war, afforded the opportunity that my mother had been waiting and praying for. She had kept a clandestine school in her house, principally for the benefit of her own children. The fact is, not many were inclined to take the trouble and risk of studying books, and all could not be trusted. But there were a few that mother could take into her confidence and who would come around and be introduced to John Comly's speller and reader. What a book it was!

It began with a. b. c: then ba, be, bi: then ab, eb, ib: then bla, ble, bli: then four letters and five. Two syllables; three, four and up to seven, with reading lessons, and illustrations scattered all thru the pages, and definitions appended.

I learned my a, b, c's forward, then backward. z, y, x, w, v, u, t, s, r, q, p, o, n, m, l, k, j, i, h, g, f,e, d, c, b, a, which I now write from memory, without stopping to consider whether it is correct or not.   I learned my letters "straight along," and learned them "skipping," and I knew them. This was the "Comly" method. The inductive, modern method has a child reading without knowing one letter from another. In other words, the modern method requires the child to look at a group of letters, and call it by a name, without at all knowing why it should be thus called. It is not so called because it sounds that, but, because it looks that. So, the child cannot give a reason for its being that, except, the teacher said so. When it sees an unfamiliar group of letters, and has not been told what the group stands for, the child cannot spell it out for itself

Even with all this, I am not prepared to denounce the new method. It has been some years since I taught school: when I did, I followed the old method, and now, I find myself pointing out the letters to my baby—she is twenty-nine months old today—and telling her what this, and that spells. Only yesterday she was walking down the street with me, and said: "look! there is c, a, t, cat." She knows the alphabet, and has been spelling phonetically for more than a year.

When mother taught me all there was in Comly's—and there was much in it—she then procured other books: at first secretly, then openly. When she taught me all that she knew, she would send me to any one in the neighborhood who would teach me more: first, secretly, but when sentiment changed, then, openly. When attention was so turned to political conditions, that the white people didn't know and didn't much care about what was going on among the Negroes, mother opened up her school out right. Some would come at night, but, the regular session was held Sunday morning before Church time, for nothing in the world would keep mother from going to Church. By the time mother could hold her school every Sunday morning without fear, I had learned enough to be her assistant teacher. So, I taught school before I went to school, technically speaking. When Lincoln was elected, before I was yet in my teens, I could write a letter for my mother to my aunts in Wilmington, Del. When freedom came, and the boys felt that they had become men sure enough, and began to court the girls in down right earnestness, they had to come to me to get their letters written. Many a time, I have written a letter, and then have been called upon by the recipient to read it.

John Comly's speller and reader had also the multiplication table and this was a part of the education of the Comly students. The fact is, by the time you knew Comly from lid to lid; the spelling and reading, and stories with moral lessons, and definitions, multiplication table and all, and could teach it to others, you knew more than some present day country school teachers holding first grade certificates.

The first comet that I remember, came about the beginning of the war. The old people called it "the star with a tail to it," and be-

lieved with all their heart that it had some
connection with the new political and social
conditions that were about us. Night after
night we would stand gazing into the heavens,
commenting on the significance of the celes-
tial stranger. Then back to the Bible and read
with peculiar unction, and interest, and faith:
"Now, when Jesus was born in Bethlehem of
Judea, behold there came wise men from the
East to Jerusalem, saying, where is He that
is born King of the Jews, for we have seen
His star in the East, and are come to worship
Him."

Had we not as much right to gaze upon our
stella phenomenon as the Eastern Magi?
Who can dare say that both stars were not
timed to direct attention to current events?
Or that events were not brought about at a
time when the star could serve as a harbinger?
Any way,, it was a time for serious thought,
and "the star with a tail" helped us to think.

Then to the Bible again, and read: "So the
King of the North shall come and cast up
a mount, and take the most fenced cities, and
the arms of the South shall not withstand."

Such passages as these, from St. Matthew,
and the prophet Daniel, taken in connection
with the presence of the comet, offered texts

for the pulpit, and subjects for the fireside, and strengthened the faith of those who were already to believe that the "King of the South" would be overcome. Superstition and emotionalism, after all, have their place in human life and action. The average slave had accepted the inevitable, and was making the most of his miserable lot. some indeed were content, and fully believed that they were created for the place that they were filling. It was so rooted and grounded in their very nature that they were inferior beings that the belief was literally transmitted to their children. Just a year or two ago, Prof. J. R. Hawkins and I secured a drawing room going South, to avoïd the horrors of the Jim Crow crib. The train stopped at a station in Virginia, and two colored lads were standing on the platform: one lifting his voice to a high pitch, exclaimed: "I don't believe dem niggers is settin in de white folk's car." It was just about "candle lighten time." So. we quietly pulled down the curtains, and put on the lights within.

So deeply branded was that sense of inferiority, and so persistently has the lesson been kept before us, that fifty years after freedom, within a few stone throws of the National

Capitol, a young Negro yet in his teens, still of school age and perhaps had been to such schools as his town afforded, seemed horrified at the presumption? of "niggers"—mind you—riding in a car that could have only been intended for "white folks."

It required signs and wonders to arouse the multitudes, and cause them to believe God, and trust "Moses and Aaron."

There were "Uncle Tom," and Richard Allen: and Christopher Jones: and Frederick Douglass: and Sojourner Truth, and others, and many like them, who always believed, or hoped, and were ready to act upon the slightest appearance of a change in conditions. But the masses were fast asleep: and why not? Three hundred years of bondage, and darkness, are quite enough to crush all the native manhood and hope out of the average soul. The only wonder is, that there were so many found that could hail the welcome morning with faith sublime, and really grasp the purpose and significance of the new order.

Is it not even a greater wonder that none became infidels, and so many accepted Christianity at the hand of masters, who were daily and hourly contradicting, and dishonoring the very religion that they taught and professed?

One need not go any further than this very fact, to prove that the doctrines of the Bible are true, and that the Christian religion is divine.

What, but truth divine could enable an undeveloped, untaught, enslaved and oppressed people to "kiss the rod that smote them," forgive the oppressor, and look forward to promised deliverance?

What, but almighty power, and truth divine, could lighten the heaviest burdens, and comfort in trouble?

Who, but God, can "lock the jaws of lions," and "quench fiery flames?" All this, and more, was the experience of the people, to whom came the boon of freedom, after the war of the rebellion.

There is a fact often referred to by statesmen and orators, but which, perhaps, has a greater significance than has been fully understood, or acknowledged.

When war was declared between the North and the South, by a sort of blinded credulity, the South believed that it could conquer; and when terms of compromise were offered, the South stubbornly refused to accept them. But it was well known that to win, meant, a gigantic effort must be put forth, that would mobilize, and draw upon the full strength of the States in rebellion. It was necessary then for practically all of the man power of the South, to go to the front, thus leaving the homes without protection.

In a few cases, slaves were taken by the masters as waiters and body servants. In some instances, they were set to work at building breast works. But nearly all were left at home, necessarily, to raise the crops. This placed the women and children at the mercy of the slaves: slave women, as well the slave men. The women had a grievance as well as the men. It would have been the easiest thing possible, for the men and the women to have made common cause, and between the kitchen and the field, to have literally exterminated their oppressors. Many of them went over the lines to the union army. They could have given a parting blow before leaving, by murderous assaults, and by the use of the torch. The men could have outraged the defenseless white women, just as their own had been outraged by white men.

Let no one think that they were too stupid to think of these things, nor, that the black man is so thoroughly unhuman, and unnatural as to be absolutely incapable of vindictiveness.

There are two ways to account for it, and only two ways. First, they were divinely, and providentially kept from the very things that retributive justice was punishing others for. They had learned to "cast their burdens on the Lord." They used to say: "that which goes over the devil's back, must come under his belly." The little that they understood as the truth of religion, and the much more, savoring of superstition that influenced their lives, said, that would not be the proper course, This made them at least stop and think before acting. But, the other reason is probably even stronger. There has always been an Elijah; a Moses, to influence and lead the people. In Africa today, the Paramount Chief controls the people by a simple code of unwritten laws, that have been transmitted from generation to generation by tradition. The English people in South Africa, to my personal knowledge, depend more on the people's chief and head men, to keep the masses of the people loyal to the crown, than they do upon the law and Army. So it was, in that critical period of our history, when the race could have forfeited its claim upon the respect and sympathy of mankind, and the favor of the al-

mighty God, their leaders came forward and
spoke the word that decided their course.

I was but a lad; too young to enlist in the
Army, or to take a very active part in things
at home, but there was not anything more
indelibly impressed upon my mind, than the
fact, that our people would go in crowds, Sunday after Sunday to the "meeting house"—
we seldom said Church—to hear what news
Father Jones had, and what advice he would
give. He would not come every Sunday. He
had his own way of doing things. He was
as Methodical in discharging religious duties,
as he was in his daily vocations. Whenever
we saw him coming we knew he had a mes-
sage. As emotional as we generally were in
religious worship there would be no thought
of "shouting" upon the days when we saw
the old prophet, with long strides wending
his way to the Sanctuary. We were all eyes
and ears for a season. I can hear his voice
now, as he emphasizes this and that precept,
and bade us beware that our own actions
did not deprive us of the divine blessing, and
guidance, and deliverance that we had come
to seek. From him, the class leaders would
take up the word, and impress it; and from

them, it would be taken up by the heads of the homes, and made fireside conversation.

These blessed old men, and precious old women, who knew God and trusted in Him and in Him alone for salvation. ceased not by night and by day, to counsel against rashness, and implore the people to patiently wait upon God.

Our people, both slave and free, were not all a common lot, on one level. There were divisions, classes and distinctions among them. They would refer to the white people as "big bugs," college bred, or poor, white trash. Just so among themselves. They were classed as industrious or lazy, "smart" or ignorant, of good or bad character. A character much despised was the deceitful "white man's nigger." He was generally persona grata at the big house, and would carry news.

On account of those distinctions, the colored folk had their society. Some free men were industrious, and made their families quite comfortable. Of course, there must be no "putting on airs." The children were expected to wear the regulation, common clothing, and go bare-foot in summer. All were expected to be "polite," bow to every person you met, and keep strictly in your place. But you might wear clean and whole clothing. To be "ragged" was a sign of poverty or laziness. To call a person, an "onery, dirty rascal," was to put him down very low.

Uncle Mike Rigby, and Solomon Hemsley, whom the boys called Sol. Tarchie—Saul of Tarsus—got into a quarrel one night, down in Crooktown. Uncle Mike was capable of showing a good deal of spunk at times, while Solomon was considered mild and easy; even too much so to work hard.

The quarrel waxed rather warm, and Uncle Mike began to say things that were not very complimentary. But Solomon, true to his good nature, even in a quarrel, took it patiently, until Uncle Mike, in a fit of passion, exclaimed: "You are a nasty, onery, good-for-nothing, dirty dog." This was more than even Sol. Tarchie could stand, and in the next moment all that was seen of Uncle Mike was a heap of much patched and now dusty clothes, crying for help; while Solomon, the victor, with both knees in the beast of his vanquished foe and slanderer, triumphantly shouted: "Uncle Mike, I will not take that from you."

Many slave men would till "patches" at night, and raise extra provisions for their families. They would hunt; catch muskrats,

coons and opossoms; sell the hides, and make
a little change for themselves and their families.   I do not know of any masters who
would object to their slaves bestowing such
extra care upon their families.   The fact is, it
helped the master to raise his "stock," but it
also exhibited a manly and worthy desire on
the part of the husband and father to make
his family as comfortable as possible.

My father was a good provider, and my
mother believed in keeping her household
clean and whole.   She would rise early and
work till late.   She made the clothing for the
family, knit the stockings, made and quilt-
ted" the bedspreads, of which there was always a plenty on hand, and sewed "carpet
rags" for home made, or rag carpets.   Dried
fruit, and put up preserves in an abudance.
Fruit was plentiful and sugar was cheap.
Uncle Jim Jones declared that John Coppin
was the luckiest man with pigs he ever saw.
When I heard Uncle Jim make that declaration about my father, even to the disparity of
his own pigs, which were "of the same litter,"
I believed it, and was rather glad to have been
the son of so lucky a father.   But, as my
mind runs back, and I discover the pigs of
Uncle Jim wading knee deep in mud and

squealing for something to eat, while the pigs of "luck" were sleeping in a warm pen with a plenty of leaves or straw for a bed, or standing at regular intervals to a well-filled trough, I conclude that the "luck" was in the care bestowed.

We boys worked on farms. There was practically nothing else to do. We went to work on the first day of March, and worked until Christmas, then came home to remain January and February. Father and mother seemed happy when, in the cold days of winter their children were about them. Those "lucky pigs" would be in the smoke house, and vegetables that were not in barrels, would be buried in heaps in the garden. We would hunt during the winter, and generally have on hand fresh game.

I remember the first dollar I earned away from home.

A farmer named Perry Pennington wanted me to help thin corn. I must have been about nine years old. My mother let me go. It was a great experience for me to be out into the field with the men, women and children; to sit at the big long table and eat with the men and listen to their jokes. Pennington had no slaves of his own. One of the hired men that

worked for him was a slave to another man,
the rest were free people. He was gentle and
kind and would joke with the men. The wife
of the slave man referred to was a free
woman, and was Pennington's cook. This
afforded an opportunity for man and wife to
be together, which was not always the case
by any means. Some slave men were permitted to visit their wives every other week.
Some, once a month. In some rare cases,
every week. In some cases, a wife would live
in an adjacent county, and some miles away.
If the master was a considerate man, he would
permit his slave to ride one of the horses on
his periodical visits to see his wife. Others
didn't care whether he went or not, just so
he answered roll call every morning.

As I remember it now, I worked a whole
week on the Pennington place, at thinning
corn. When Saturday afternoon came he
handed me a gold dollar. These coins were in
circulation then. It was so small that I feared
that I might lose it. So, I wrapped it up in
a small bit of paper and carried it in my hand
until I reached home, and handed it to father.
I can even now realize how proud I was to
have actually earned a gold dollar. Granting
that I worked a week, I earned a little over

sixteen cents per day and my board. But, the experience! It was my first sight upon the real outside world, where there were large groups of people, and big barns, and herds of cattle, and apple orchards, with now and then a chance to ride horseback. I would not have begrudged paying sixteen cents a day for such privileges as the experience afforded. But, added to all of this I actually had owned a gold dollar, and could present it to father with a feeling of self-importance such as I had never before experienced.

After this, I often went to the Pennington farm for a job, especially at harvest time, when boys were needed to "pick up sheaves."

At the age of twelve I went on the fourth day of April to help a farmer by the name of Francis King, plant corn. I remained with him the balance of the year. He gave me twenty dollars and a suit of clothes for the nearly ten months. It was from there I went with Billy Cannon—Mr. King's grandson—to Freeman's Mill, at the head of the Sassafras River. Francis King was a big, fat man, who had been married four times. He did not own slaves, but hired both slave and free labor. His youngest child, a boy, was named Thomas Alabone. This was in 1860. Alabone was about seven years old, I suppose. When, in 1881, I went to take charge of Bethel Church, Baltimore, I found the Rev. Thomas A. King pastoring a church there; of course we were glad to meet each other.

My father always allowed his boys to select their own places of work, but mother saw to it that the bargain was all right. The farmer must promise to give so much for the term; a plenty to eat, and a suit of clothes that could not be characterized as, shall-I-go-naked-before spring. My father would sometimes wince and become embarrassed as mother stood "laying down the law" to the man who was hiring her boy. A pair of boots—winter boots—was always included in the phrase "and his clothes."

The next man I hired to was named Eldridge. This was in 1861. He bargained to give me thirty-two dollars and my clothes for ten months, March to Christmas. By this time I as becoming a regular, and at the same time was making a unique reputation as the boy who could read and write. This was considered marvelous. I would read the Bible, and hymns from a hymn book which my brother-in-law, John Bayard, gave me. This service I would perform for the older men

and women who cared for it. For the boys
I would read from story books and illustrated
comic tales, and kiss verses, much to the
amusement of the lads who would gather
about me around the big fireplace.

I think my mother never charged her pupils
anything for instruction. she seemed so anxious to have them learn. But when the boys
began to come to me to have their love letters
written I began to charge them ten cents a
letter. This they gladly paid.

While at the Eldridge farm I had an experience in school teaching that I never had before nor since. Uncle "Kit—Christopher—
Cain" was a chunky, little, bow-legged, pine-
knot man, of the Guinea type. He would not
comb his hair, for he said, "the loss of every
knot was equal to an ounce of sense." He
had a sharp chin, which grew a beard about
four inches long. This Uncle Kit plaitted and
seemed to regard it as a sort of tribal mark
of distinction; but, comb that head he
wouldn't. His wife, Aunt Rose, could beat
him two to one for queer looks, in general
make-up, and besides was cock-eyed and left-
handed. They were "Simon pure" Africans,
of equatorial hue. They had a daughter, to
whom they gave the name Rosebud. The only

thing suggestive I could see in the chosen name was, she was typically a bud from the old bush.

Well, Uncle Kit, who considered himself very smart at "high dictionary" wanted Rosebud taught to read and write, and my services were engaged to perform what proved to be an impossible task, with the promise of five dollars when the work was completed.

It was doubtful from the beginning of my success with the chip-of-the-old-block, but I never had the least suspicion that I would ever get five dollars for it.

The food on the farm was very plain and monotonous, and with a careless cook, was often very unpalatable.

As Uncle Kit, Aunt Rose and Rosebud lived upstairs to themselves, and as Aunt Rose was the cook, she would pilfer such food as she wished to have for her private family and cook it after night came. Now, as my school would be held upstairs, in the Cain quarters, I knew I would be good for a toothsome supper every night. So, I closed the bargain, and began work. I worked faithfully for about three months, and finding that I could not succeed in making Miss Rosebud understand even so much as the alphabet, I closed the school for the term," but really with no intention of ever again opening out at "Cainville."

When Uncle Kit found out that I did not re-open school, he denounced me as being not worth my salt, and would say: "What good is edication to some people? Now there is Levi Coppin, an edicated boy: I promised to give him five dollars to larn my Rosybud to read and write, but do you think he would do it? He jist teached her a little while, den got tired and stopped; had he kept on, Rosybud would have been readin' and writin', and he would have had his five dollars!"

Not one word of either proposition in the conclusion was true. "Rosybud" could not be taught to read and write, and even if she could have, Uncle Kit never would have paid five dollars for the job; for if he ever told the truth in all his life, I think it was by accident.

Freedom came shortly afterwards. Uncle Kit died in a few years. Aunt Rose found another companion who lived with her for a time, and then forsook her and "took up" with Rosebud.

It is well known that when war was first declared, colored men where not taken into the army. But the purposes of God could not be defeated. It was soon apparent to the

North that the Negro was needed to help win the war. At first, Lincoln would "preserve" the Union with or without emancipating the slaves, but at the last, he found out that the only way to preserve the Union was by permitting the slaves to fight for its preservation.

Imagine the feelings of our people at the first sight of colored men in soldier's uniform! When the call was made general, many responded. When later on, a recruiting office was opened in Cecilton by Lieutenant Brown, some of our boys who had joined the army were selected to come, now as soldiers, to their own home, and induce others to enlist. Under "shoulder arms," they would march through the little village, "as proud as Lucifer" and without fear.

While Lieutenant Brown and his men remained, many volunteered. Some slaves, whose masters still held them in bondage, came to the recruiting office, enlisted and placed themselves under the protection of the flag. They were called "United States Colored Troops." No such distinctions are now made between our boys fighting in France. They are not there as colored troops but as United States soldiers.

We came out of the Civil War with one commissioned officer, Major Martin R. Delaney, but we entered this world war with nearly a thousand.

When the colored soldier came, it left no doubt as to whether or not freedom had come.

Father Jones was promptly on hand with Lincoln's proclamation, but there was no one present with authority to say to the slave, you are free; so all were in suspense.

Uncle Jim Jones drove his mistress to Cecilton, and some one, a white person, told him that he was free now, and it was discretionary with him whether or not he drove the carriage back. When Uncle Jim reached home he informed every one of what he had heard. When a few evenings after that, his old master himself drove the carriage to town and was late returning, Uncle Jim, in order to make a test case, would not remain to unharness the horses, but said, in a way that his master would be sure to hear it: "There has got to be a new understanding," which "new understanding" came promptly the next morning when "Mars Frankie" approached him to know about the strange doctrine which he was preaching around the place. Poor Uncle

Jim begged pardon, saved his back, and said no more about a "new understanding."

He was too old to be very independent. He continued to live in the little house on the place, and work for Marse Frankie, who paid him about what he thought his services were worth. He never was able to throw off the terrible fear he always had of his master, who, by the way, was never cruel to him ; but, he finally mustered enough courage to go and come at will.

It was a great thing to him, even so near the end, to rise in the morning and say he did not feel like going to work, and so, remain at home.

Uncle Jim was among the men called "wicked." Not indeed of the "Perry Thompson" type, spoken of in another chapter. But one who could swear profanely, drink whiskey and never go near the church. A really "hardened sinner." But, when freedom came, he went to Wilmington, Del., to visit some relatives. On Orange Street, near Tenth, stood an iron foundery, where Uncle Jim, saw for the first time in his life an exhibition of "hot lead" running like water. He had always heard that Satan poured such down the throat of sinners who died in sin. He had all his life entertained a lingering doubt as to whether lead could be made into a liquid. But when he saw the real, red stuff running in a stream, doubt was turned into "conviction for sin," and he came home a changed man; united with the church, and remained faithful to death. He got into a quarrel after that with a white man who cursed him. Uncle Jim said: "You need not think I am afraid to cuss you back, it is only because I belong to meetin'. "

May it be ever remembered that there were families, even among the slave-holding class, who were kind to their people, and to colored people in general. Some had a real affection for individuals for various reasons. Some times it was the nurse, or, "black mammy" about whom we have heard so much. Some times it was a friendship that grew up between persons, about the same age, and who grew up together as chums. In this way we can account for the mysteriously learning to read on the part of many. There were cases approaching, at least, the David and Jonathan friendship. where "Jonathan" would tell what was being said at the great house, would give food and clothing to his friend, and secretly teach him how to read and count: who in his heart sympathised with his friend in bondage, and no doubt thought, what Lincoln once said: "If ever I get a chance to hit this thing I will hit it d——— hard." But there were also persons naturally kind of heart, who sympathized with the oppressed, and disliked oppression.

I have in mind now a master who would not strike one of his slaves,—they often deserved it—nor suffer any one else to do so. I also have in mind a man who had no slaves, and who was ever ready to give warning to the Colored people of any impending danger, and who helped many slaves to escape by conducting them personally to an under Ground Rail Road Station. I do not speak now of the well known class of Abolitionists who were the forerunners of a political party, and who were known, dreaded and fought by the slave holding class. I speak of individuals who were never known in public life, and who, in many instances felt that they could not afford to have their attitude known. They did not choose the John Brown method, but were glad enough, when, by some other means, a rebellion was brought about.

Many slave holders manumitted their slaves. This indeed accounts for a large number of free Negroes. But this practice was finally forbidden by law, and those who found themselves inheriting the human chattel, must keep them, or pass them over to others by sale or presents: even traded for cattle. Some were set "levy free." I do not know the origin of this term, but it was used by the old people to describe a person who had been turned loose by word of mouth, without any legal process. Perhaps the object was to avoid violating the law that forbade manumitting, and still give the slave the benefit of a sort of freedom.

I have elsewhere referred to the Cruikshank family as being humane and kind.

The family consisted of the father, Francis; the mother, Mary; four sons, viz: John Chandler; George Washington; Francis, Jr.—and Henry Harrison. And one daughter, Mary, named for her mother. These people, the whole of them, were cultured, gentle and belonged to the "gentry" class.

John Chandler was a merchant, succeeding his father. George Washington was a farmer, but afterwards a lawyer and editor. Francis studied for the Episcopal ministry, but went South during the war, and died of Yellow fever Henry Harrison became a physician. Practiced at his home town, Cecilton, for a time. Got

married, and finally moved to Johnstown, Pa.
He was absent during the great flood, but arrived in time to see his family swept away,
which sight set him crazy.

What of the daughter, Mary? The father,
Francis made a goodly fortune as a merchant,
and gave over the business to his son Chandler;
purchased a farm, built a modern house and
moved with his wife and only daughter to this
country place.

The war set free the four slaves they owned,
and all the people on the farm were hired
help. This was after the Proclamation, and
before the surrender. My father had purchased a piece of ground, and built a house on it.
This was adjacent the Cruikshank place.

There had always existed a sort of friendship between "Miss Mary Cruikshank" and
my mother. Mother used to work for her, especially on "house cleaning" occasions. "Miss
Mary" would give her many things for the
children. Toys, and occasionally articles of
clothing. But best of all, books, that her children had finished and laid aside. These constituted the nucleus of my first library.

When both families moved, and lived close
together, the intercourse between them became quite general. In 1864, a year before

the close of the war, I went to work on the Francis Cruikshank farm, adjoining which was the one farmed by his son George Washington. They were the same as one farm in a way. We would work on first the one, and then the other.

Public sentiment and political conditions had under gone such a change by this time, that any one who felt disposed to teach a colored person to read, could do so without hazard. This was my opportunity. It would seem that my life had been converging to this point. Miss Mary, the daughter, was one of those saintly characters who seemed by nature to have been born from above. She embodied a combination of all the good qualities of her parents, and besides, she was an exemplary Christian.

I was not on the place long before she offered to give Bible lessons to any of the boys who cared to so devote some of their evening hours.

I accepted the offer at once, and induced some of the other boys to do likewise. This continued for a few nights only, however, when the school dwindled down to Jim Jones, Jr., and myself, and then to me only.

But "Missie" as we called her, not at all discouraged, gave all her attention to the one pupil who continued, and besides, the studies were divided between the Bible and secular studies. This is what I so much needed at that very time. I had about completed Comly's text book, and besides, had gone about as far as my mother could carry me. But "Missie" had been to college, and she was ready with any proposition in advance studies. So night after night, and month after month, I was the solitary student in this Biblico—secular school, which was doing more for me than I was at all able at that time to understand.

But besides this—and strange too to say—George Washington, the really brainy member of the Cruikshank family, was not married at the time, and feeling lonesome, invited me to spend as many evenings as I wished with him. It is more than likely that his sister had spoken to him of my faithfulness, and aptness as a student, and he, being of her spirit gave me a chance to divide the time with him. He was of like spirit of his sister as to kindness, but was not much on religious subjects. His mind ran toward law, and he had not calculated on spending many years as farmer, but had his mind on Elkton, the county seat, and the practice of law. He finally went from Elkton to Baltimore, and edited a daily paper, called: "The Day."

He took a different course with me as a student. He would read, and explain what he had read, and force me into discussions. I can see now that he was really practicing on me, as a student minister does on a congregation. I was his audience, or jury, to whom he would speak, and explain. I would ask him questions. When in my course of reading, I came to words that I could not pronounce, or words and sentences that I did not understand, I would take them to him. He seemed to take the greatest delight in having me come with hard propositions. Hard indeed to me, but not to him.

I never heard him swear: he often used the word: "by George." When he was especially pleased with a nights work, he would sometimes say: "by George, Levi, you are going to be a smart chap." After I was grown and in the ministry, and he, established in his chosen field of work, I met him on the train between Philadelphia and Baltimore. It was indeed a pleasant reunion. We discussed sure enough then. He wanted to draw me out on my theological ideas. Among the many things he asked me was, what became of men who die without an opportunity to hear the Gospel. Of course I gave him the cut and dried answer about the heathen being a law unto himself, and how he was provided for by the atonement. I dare say he anticipated me, and quickly replied: "well, since the heathen can be saved without being civilized, why not let him alone? for many, after being civilized, will be lost." This he said too, to draw me out. I asked him if he would rather be a heathen, living in the blissfulness of ignorance, than a Baltimore editor, with the knowledge of how to be saved. We called it even and quit.

The war finally came to a close by the surrender of Lee and the fall of Richmond. There was no longer any doubt then about the final issue. Slavery, the "sum of all villainy" was crushed. Its ghost has appeared in different and many forms since General Lee gave up the struggle on the field of battle; but, at most, it is but a ghost of the personality that lived and florished so long, and caused so much sorrow and degradation. The results of slavery had become so much a part of our civilization, both in Church and State, that there is no wonder that a written declaration could not wipe it out instanta. It required years for it to grow into the giant that it became, and its final and total obliteration will be by the growth of Christian sentiment, with other contributing causes.

But let us thank God, that legalized servitude is dead and doomed. The Amendments to the Constitution that fixed its status, will not only remain, but other amendments will be added; to emancipate women, to make impossible legalized vice, and give our struggling humanity a better chance to reach its highest and best possibilities.

The Small pox broke out at our home. Its origin was never known. But, since it was coming, it had to begin some where. I had heard much about small pox, and knew that people dreaded it, as they dread maddogs. Theoretically, I know about the isolation caused by it, but I was never close to it.

It came suddenly and unexpectedly, of course. No preparation had been made for a siege such as it would cause.

As soon as it became known, no one would dare come near the place. But this is both law and custom, and nothing else is expected at such a time. My friend David Anderson would come within calling distance, in the big field beyond, and we would converse at a distance, and he would leave what we had arranged for him to bring. This was always at night. Uncle Jim Jones lived on an adjacent lot on the Cruikshank property. This made us such close neighbors, that the public would be as much afraid of one from his family as from ours. So his place was also under quarantine.

Our dear old family doctor who had been the only doctor in the family from the birth of the first child—Doctor Roberts—had passed away, and we sent for Dr. Harry Cruikshank. He had not been long out of school and was but slowly building up a practice. A young doctor in the country, and especially at that time, certainly had to serve a probation, before being fully trusted. While Dr. Roberts lived, we would not think of sending for any other physician in time of sickness. This was also the prevailing sentiment of the place, and of the times.

This was an opportunity for Dr. Harry to try his skill, and also to make a reputation for himself: for I tell you, any Doctor who could cure small pox, would soon make a reputation in Cecil County.

When Dr. Harry came and pronounced the case small pox, he proceeded to vaccinate all the other members of the family.

I just happened to have been at the house and was caught in the quarantine. Some how I got an idea that my presence there was providential, and that God intended that I should minister to the rest of the family. With this thought in view, I decided not to attempt to assist the Almighty by keeping myself from catching the dreaded complaint, so I refused to be vaccinated.

Every day when Dr. Harry would come he would ask if I were ready for the operation, and I would promptly answer in the negative. He could not do it alone by force, and no one or no number of persons would have volunteered their assistance.

I never told him why I refused, but, whether I acted wisely or unwisely, I made the matter a case of faith and prayer. I reasoned, that if God indeed wanted me to perform the service of nursing the others he would keep me well to do it. Father was just recovering from a spell of sickness: he didn't take it. But one after another of the family went down under it; and it also spread to the next

house where were four in family, who took
it. I alone was left on my feet to cut wood
and carry water, and cook for two families.
Mother, who had but a light case of it, was
soon able to assist me.

When the Doctor saw that his vaccinated
subjects went down and I did not, he called
me a wonder.

All the patients got well except dear old
uncle Jim Jones. He died, and, assisted by
his son Jim, who had recovered, I buried him
under the apple tree in the garden. I made
a coffin out of some pieces of board, and, acting as grave digger, and undertaker and parson, I laid him to rest with simple ceremony.
He died in the faith. Peace to his ashes!

Henry Jones, one of the three Jones boys
was among those who enlisted under Lieutenant Brown, and was a color sergeant, in the
19th Maryland, U. S. Colored troops. He was
mustered out at the close of the war and returned home. The Jones family consisted of
eight children: George: Martha: James: Henry: Delia: Mary: Emma and Frank. They
all, taking the condition of their mother, were
free born. "When the cruel war was over and
the Soldiers had returned," there was a general readjustment of things.

The colored people could have their meetings regularly, and go and come without asking permission.

They would invite the white people now and hold protracted meetings. The old people called them "pertracterable" meetings.

In the fall of the year, good old Friendship would be a veritable battle ground for several weeks. Getting religion, was by way of the mourners' bench, and that was the only way we knew about. We had looked from the gallery in the "Old Brick Church," and witnessed how the white folks came forward to the mourners' bench while Sylvester Stephens led in singing: "Turn to the Lord and Seek Salvation," and how the mourners "came through." It would be quite a useless waste of time to try to convince the old people that you "had religion" if you had not been to the mourners' bench and prayed until you got through.

Some of them were quite adepts at the business. They would back slide and then have to come back and get religion over again.

Moses Cain, a brother to Rosebud could be depended upon to furnish the meeting with at least one mourner, for he was sure to back-

slide at some time during the year. Like the
seed sown in stony ground, he could not stand
the scorching sun of temptation. This was
especially true about harvest time, when every
body was jolly, and there was feasting at the
kitchen and a whole barrel of whiskey in the
harvest field. "Moses" would indulge too freely and fall by the way. But when the meetings
would begin, and it would be noised abroad
that they were "having great times at Friendship," Moses would "arise and go to his father.'
Those who had often seen him "come through"
knew that it would not be altogether safe to
be near him when he ended the final struggle.
The first time that I witnessed it, I was standing close to Uncle Alfred Bacon, who said to
me : "you had better move, for Mose is going
to get up from there "terrectly." And he did.
And so did the benches that were near him ;
and so did the stove pipe, when the stove was
so shaken that it nearly fell. When he had
rolled quite the length of the building, sweep-
ing everything before him, he would get up
return to the Band, and join in with the singing, hand clapping, and swaying of the body
that was characteristic of "pertracterble"
meetings.

All this was due to slavery and all of its accompanying evils. A just judge took the will for the deed, and fixed the modicum of responsibility. At the great Judgement Bar, all will be judged impartially, the oppressed and the oppressor.

Conditions and sentiment so changed during the war, and especially near the close, that it was thought safe to organize a Sunday School; ostensibly for the purpose of religious instruction, but principly for the purpose of giving to those who wished it, an opportunity to learn to read. Dear old Friendship was available for this purpose, and soon the little sanctuary, that had been the scene of all kinds of religious meetings, and every degree of emotionalism, was now vocal with new and strange sounds. Behold, they spell! Behold, they read! Behold, they Study! Men and women as well as lads and lasses. Men past fifty, in a primary class with children not yet in their teens, learning the alphabet, and that which followed according to the Comly method.

My mother felt that her special work was accomplished. She had been solitary and alone, the John the Baptist crying in the Wilderness, and not crying too loudly for fear of being apprehended, but crying persistently, and with hope. She had not only awakened a desire to learn, but had kept it alive, until with inconceivable suddenness the opportunity to satisfy the desire, came. But more, she had done what was farthest from her thought; she had actually created a teacher for the emergency: for who was so well prepared to be first professor at "Friendship Institute," as the gift of Santa Claus, upon whom she had bestowed so much anxious care, with only the support of blind faith. Draw on your imagination, reader, and see if you can comprehend a mother's joy, standing face to face with such an acheivement.

Mother showed no disposition to go to the new place of meeting and take part as a teacher. There were still a few of her old pupils who preferred the quiet and seclusion of the fireside to which they had gone when no one from without suspected the purpose. This feeling perhaps, was shared by those who felt that they were slow and backward; or even a little fearful and afraid that the Union Arms might not be ultimately successful.

In this new enrollment would be persons from every direction. Many who by various means had learned their letters, and even how to read, would be on the new register. It is rather surprising how many persons of this class turned up. Each was a surprise to the other. There were not any, to be sure, who had gone to any considerable extent. Each one who could at all spell and read constituted a sort of wonder, in view of the prohibitory laws that were in existence.

At this time there came a man from Baltimore, Horace Brown by name, I know nothing of his pedigree, or how he came into possession of his book learning, but among us he was indeed a star of the first magnitude. He had a good English education. Was young strong and enthusiastic. He came just in the nick of time. Indeed, his coming could not have been better timed, had it been in answer to a call.

Being facile princeps, no one questioned his right to take full charge as Principal. The school grew in numbers, until Friendship was too small to accommodate those who came. It was like a flock of thirsty cattle discovering a pond of water and making a mad rush to drink. There was a great demand for Comly's speller and Reader for those who had to begin at the beginning and these constituted an overwhelming majority. For those who were prepared for higher studies, Prof. Brown provided suitable books.

This was the first school in Cecil County in which colored people could openly learn to read and write, and being held on Sundays only, it afforded but one day in a week for study. But it was the harbinger of what was soon to follow. It was the big bright morning star ushering in the day. It was a clarion note to the intellectually blind, to come and receive sight. Hitherto, only the few, whose indomitable nature inspired a thirst for knowledge, that was stronger than the fear of chains, or even death itself, could succeed in satisfying this thirst in part: but now, the door is thrown open to all who care to come. To all, at least, who are within easy reach of the open door of opportunity. The decisive battle had not yet been fought at Appomattox, but the passing breezes whispered that the end was near, and only the faint-hearted and indifferent would wait for further evidence of the good time coming, or refuse to grasp the golden privileges already at hand.

CHAPTER IV.

After the Civil War.

"All is well that ends well," says the old adage. Even war, I suppose: tho it may be very much as the rugged old Ohio General discribed it as being.

Without a doubt, war is terrible, viewed from any standpoint. Frederick Douglass spoke of it as: filling the land with "widows and orphans, and the shadow of death." Young and innocent lives, not at all responsible for it, must be destroyed by it. But so long as there is evil in the moral world, there will be strife among men. The war of the sixties did not differ from other wars as to cause. No one thing can be named as alone causing such social upheavals, but there is always some principal thing. In this case, it was slavery. The seceding States claimed the right to buy,

and sell and own, and work human beings as
slaves, without any interference on the part
of the other states forming the Union.   The
states that elected Abraham Lincoln, claimed
that the majority of the States had a right to
legislate for the minority when an evil threat-
ened the wellbeing of the whole people. Slavery was regarded by the "Union" people, as
being such an evil.

The slogan was not: "shall slavery be destroyed," but: "shall the Union be preserved."
It is generally thought, that Mr. Lincoln,
partly from a lack of courage, and partly for
policy sake, held out the "Union" theory. "I
must save the Union," was his cry: "with or
without the destruction of slavery."

There was not another moral question on
the surface, that could not have been settled
at the polls, without going to war; or, that
could not have been settled by compromise
after the bloody conflict began. Slavery was
the real bone of contention. Its abolition was
prophesied in the event of Lincoln's election,
and the prophecy continued after his election
before he made any declaration concerning it.
It was expected of him. He expected it of
himself, and so, gathered about him as an
official family those who held like views. It

was in the air. The time was ripe to strike the blow. It was God's time. Never did men shoulder arms for a more righteous cause, and never did men under arms feel more assured that their cause was righteous. The monster that had strutted, and thrived, and boasted so long was doomed.

But, all were glad when it was over. Of course the Union people, like all victors, were glad that they won their cause. But, it was not long until the South realized that the destruction of slavery, was the destruction of their own greatest foe. Slavery enslaved and degraded every thing it touched. Many of the master class who were afflicted by it, realized this fact: but how to get rid of it was the trying question. It is now as then: race prejudice, and all of its attendent evils, is as a canker on the body politic. It must be especially annoying to those professing Christianity. To despise, or in any way harm a human being solely on account of his race affiliations, is cruel and unreasonable, and finds no sanction in Christian ethics. Let us hope that as American slavery was smothered in the baptism of blood, so may hateful, ungodly race and color prejudice be swept away by the death dealing devices of the present war that destroy without discrimination. Since it has become necessary to make common cause, in order to establish democracy, may it ever hereafter be considered unmanly, and unpatriotic to return to those unrighteous practices that more than any thing else made our fair land and country undemocratic.

When "the cruel war was over and the Soldiers were discharged" the work of reconstructing, and readjusting began in many ways.

Father Jones, the old prophet was promptly on hand, to instruct and guide the enthusiastic masses, intoxicated with joy, and liable at any moment to bring on trouble by acts of indiscretion. The joy was unbounded among our people. There was not the slightest difference in this respect, between the slaves and the free people. Slavery saw to it, that one code of laws governed slave and free alike, and kept those who were nominally free within the proscribed limits of the slaves.

Besides the loud acclamations of joy expressed in shouting and singing, and general hurrahs, the newly emancipated people gave vent to their feelings by going freely from place to place—a delightful privilege—and feasting, and dancing, and making merry. "The dead was alive, and the lost was found."

It is fair to suppose that every body took some part in the general merry making, but, the religious ones sought the Church as being the proper place to go, and rejoice, by giving thanks to Him, toward whose throne above their prayers had been so long directed, and dear old Friendship soon became the centre of attraction. It is now genuinely the Ecclesia, and must, for a time at least, be the forum for all matters of discussion, moral, religious, civil and intellectual.

But here a grave question confronted the people, which must be settled, and settled at once. It was a question of ownership. Uncle Perry Hinson had built Friendship on his ground, and for a time, perhaps during his life time he was recognized "head of the Church" for peace sake. After he died, the people continued to meet and worship there without any one particular exercising any special authority. But, as the "white" Church in the town was Methodist, and had really gone so far as to appoint class leaders for the colored people, it was just taken for granted that Friendship was a Methodist Church. And so, in the work of reconstruction, the minister from the "Brick

Church"—Methodist Episcopal—came down, preached at an afternoon service to the people and began to instruct them as to their duties and privileges as Methodists. This raised another question. Father Jones, who had never actually joined Friendship, and come under the domination of the M. E. Church, instructed the people to say, they did not want to belong to the Methodist Episcopal Church. Indeed! Upon what has this Caesar been feeding? If you come not to us, to whom will you go?

This brings us face to face with another important item of ecclesiastical history. The war closed in 1865; but the African Methodist Episcopal Church seceded from the M. E. organically in 1816. It had been a denomination, full fledged for 49 years, when freedom was declared. Established in Philadelphia, it had stealthily made its way here and there into nearby slave territory. Maryland being right on the line of Pennsylvania, some Allenites had crept over, and quietly organized under the A. M. E. Discipline. Such was the case at a place nine miles from Cecilton, just beyond the Bohemia River, and called Bohemia Manor. Here Father Jones held his membership.

George Mercer was the prominent man at the A. M. E. Church "On the Manor" as we said, much as was Christopher Jones at Cecilton.

"We want to be African Methodists:" was the answer given to the minister from the M. E. Church. African Methodists! What has not been going on in the darkness! "Have those rebellious Allenites been down here with their mischievous doctrine about equality, and brotherhood?" They had not been down there. The laws of the state forbade the coming and going of free Negroes in and out of the State. No one was telling the King's secrets to the Israelites, but there was "a prophet in Israel."

"You may go to the Allenites but you cannot take that Church property." Shall we indeed be deprived of this our dearest possession? Here our fathers and mothers have prayed and hoped. Here we their children have sought and found the God of our fathers. Back here on the other side of the lot, sleep our dear ones. Under the window here on the west side is the marble slab which marks the place that is sacred to the memory of "Aunt Moria Sisco" which is perhaps, the only tomb stone of the kind in the county; certainly the only one

of its kind in the Sassafras Neck. Shall indeed
this our "Ark of the Covenant" be taken by
these uncircumsized Philistines who deny the
brotherhood? Alas! Some would rather remain in the camp of the Philistines than loose
the Ark.

When the M. E. preacher's Committee went
to Elkton the County Seat, to examine the
title, and ascertain who indeed were the rightful owners of Friendship and the acre of
ground upon which it stands, it was found
that there was no record of it at all, and the
Court of Equity decided, that peacable possession for twenty years gave it to the congregation that worshipped there.

This meant great rejoicing at Friendship:
but it also meant a special sermon from the old
prophet who had safely guided them in their
first struggle under the banner of freedom.
The text: "Tell me, O thou whom my soul
loveth, where thou feedest; where thou mak-
est thy flock to rest at noon: for why should
I be as one that turneth aside by the flock
of thy companion."

When he had finished, describing the flock,
the shepherd and the sheep, we were all willing to pronounce it an effort that was worthy

the reputation of one of the greatest preachers of ante bellum times.

The next step to be taken was to make Friendship, indeed and in truth, an African Methodist Church.

Bishop Alexander Washington Wayman like Frederick Douglass—both from the famous Eastern Shore—had already been before the public long enough to have gained considerable notoriety as a leading man of the race and a noted speaker.

After Mr. Lincoln's Proclamation, and while those who might have otherwise given trouble were busy with the affairs of the war, quite a number of men came out of hiding and got about quite a good deal, preaching, lecturing, and in a general way helping the abolition movement. Prominently among them were, Frederick Douglass, Henry Highland Garnett and Alexander Wayman. All three of these "bright lights" were Marylanders. There were many others, not so widely known as these, because they did not travel as much, nor so far away from home. But they were active workers on the "Under Ground Rail Road," and were the first to come forward with a helping hand to the freedman at a time when he most needed suggestion and guidance.

Robert Purvis: William Still: Bishops J. P. Campbell and John M. Brown. Henry Gordon: Isaiah C. Wears, Stephen Smith who made quite a fortune as lumber merchant, and founded the home for the Aged and Infirm Colored people in Philadelphia, giving the munificent sum of two hundred thousand dollars. These and many others are among the number, worthy of special mention, who belong to the period under consideration.

So soon as the way opened, Bishop Wayman started South, with the cry: "I seek my brethren." Genesis xxxvii 16. Father Jones, who was on the alert, sent for him to come to Cecilton and receive Friendship and her members into the fold of African Methodism. What a day! A summer day. Early summer. When harvest fields were just becoming golden, and fruit trees were rejoicing in anticipation of crops that would soon be ready for the market. Birds were nesting and making the forest vocal with their sweet songs. The proud grove in front of Friendship was looking its best. All nature was ready for the great event. Grove Neck; Veasey's Neck; Hackspoint Neck; all the Necks united with Sassafras Neck to prove to the "Bushup" that it was well worth his while to place "Union

Bethel" as the Church was afterwards called, in the calendar of African Methodism. They came, they came; they were there.

Of course, the church would not begin to hold the people. The old regulars were there early, and on the inside. Jones', Bacons, Wilsons, Piners, Kennards, Scotts, Wrights, Youngs, Govens, Trustys, Freemans, Halls, Siscos, Crawfords, et al. My mother was there!

"Give me a chair," said the Bishop. And, placing it just inside the door, where, standing on it he could maintain a commanding view of the multitudes in the grove, as well as those who were packed like sardines in a box on the inside. With sonorous voice he began to read his text: "Blessed is the man that walketh not in the council of the ungodly," etc. We heard that day about the Godly man, and how he prospered, and the ungodly, and how like chaff he was ultimately blown away. We heard how righteousness exalteth and sin debases. Of the door of opportunity newly opened. What of divine blessing we might expect if we walked uprightly and how surely failure would come if we did not. We looked and listened; we listened and looked. The "little fat man," as he termed himself in his lecture on the "Galaxy of Bishops," did not look like any of our own men. He wore his hair long and brushed it back without parting it. His skin was as smooth as that of a woman. His face beamed with intelligence. His features were prominent, with nothing of the depression characteristic of slave conditions. He was princely in appearance, and may have been a lineal descendant from a royal house in Africa, for he was of unmixed blood. As a speaker he was naturally eloquent, with an easy style. He could preach three times a day without "soiling" his collar. Upon examination his diary showed that he averaged a sermon a day, year after year. He was much sought by white congregations, especially on camp-meeting occasions. He was conservative in speech and action. Took no prominent part in anti-slavery agitation, nor in reconstruction work. Just worked along evangelistic lines, and at that he seemed never to tire.

The vote was taken, the Friendship congregation became African Methodist, and subsequently, with Bohamia Manor and Chesapeake City, became a circuit. It is now a station, with parsonage and hall on the church lot, and

is among the most pleasant appointments on
"the Shore."

It now being settled that we had a church
which was our very own, a constituent of a
well-organized and growing denomination, entitled to a "preacher in charge" like they had at
the M. E. Church, where we had been sitting in
the gallery, having no part in the services or
government, we must apply to the Annual
Conference for a minister, and affect an in-
ternal organization, with trustees, stewards,
and the whole machinery of a well-ordered
church. We would now have our own class
leaders, who in addressing us would say
brother and sister, according to the prevailing custom in the Methodist family. Class
leaders, who would visit our homes, and, in
times of sorrow, give words of comfort. We
would now have our children baptized, and
give them names. Call them "John Wesley,"
and "Richard Allen," and "Abraham Lincoln"
if we wished. Give our daughters and sons
in marriage. Recognize the relation of par-
ent and child, and grand child, and brother and
sister. Hold revival meetings without having
white intruders come in and throw packages
of red pepper in the stove to set us all cough-
ing. Have religious and business meetings

without the presence of a town official to take an account of what was said and done.

With such blessings, and privileges, it was now time to set the house in order morally, and spiritually. There were those among us who in morals and religion were absolutely above suspicion. But a good deal of drift wood had floated down from the old condition just coming to a close; this must be given attention.

One of the most prevalent evils of Quarter life was the "Common Law Marriage" which was no marriage at all. All of the free people who cared to do so, could find some one authorized to perform the marriage ceremony, and, in most cases, it was done. But, in the happy-go-lucky custom that was so prevalent, many just "took up" with each other. In the case of slaves, no marriage would be permissible without the consent of the master; and, as many masters would not object to their slaves living as man and wife without being married, it was not at all an unusual thing for them to do so. With reference to the master giving consent, there was one exception to the rule. When a free man wished to marry a slave woman, it was good policy for the slave holding interests to con-

sent to it. Of such a union, the children
would be slave. Besides, the father, being
free, could help support the children, and the
wife also. It often happened that when a
free man chose a slave woman, for a wife, it
was that he might either purchase her freedom, or secure it by "running away" with her.
I regret to say that there were some worth-
less, heartless ones, who might select a slave
woman, because he would not be responsible
for the keep of his family. But such a one
generally got what he so richly deserved. The
wife's master would rope him in, make him
work, and give him about what he chose: thus,
he would be on a level with those of the
other slaves. At all events, the close of the
war found many living together without being married. My mother became a self-constituted missionary to such, and so soon as
our minister came, mother began gathering
up all who were irregular in their connubial
relations, and arranging with the minister for
quiet weddings. The license did not cost much
and contracting parties, even to this day, very
seldom give the minister much. It was pa-
thetic to see old people who had lived for years
as man and wife; who had children and grand
children, going to have the marriage ceremony

performed. So long as the neglect was from
no fault of theirs, it made no difference to
man; and a just God did not hold them morally responsible. But now, according to my
mother's theory it was a case of: "arise and
shine for thy light has come."   Then again,
there was father Jones, who, even in the presence of death, would not spare those who
through carelessness and indifference refused
to have the sacred and divine rite of marriage
performed.

Then there were other kinds of irregular
living by Church members when there was no
one to prefer "charges and complaints", and
bring the transgressor to book. A man might
be a member of the Church, and yet be "stopping" with a woman to whom he was not
married. Or, in the irregular union, the woman might be the Church member. These
are cases where even Common law marriage
was not claimed. Both parties going for single. The man just a "star boarder." But, in
this general clean up at Friendship, under the
new regime, such parties had to choose between getting married, or facing charges for
immoral conduct. Under the old condition of
things, stealing was not considered a crime
sufficient to: "exclude one from the Kingdom

of grace and glory." Elsewhere I have called attention to the fact, that in the moral
code of the master, stealing was not a crime
on the part of the slave, unless he stole from
his master. Of course, it was not very difficult
for the slave to add an amendment, and extend the privilege to any barn yard, or hen
roost whatsoever.

Then, there was the whiskey drinking habit.
No slave was taught that drunkenness was a
crime, and, at harvest time, the beverage
flowed freely, and every body drank, and,
"when whiskey is in, wit is out," and vulgarity
and profanity may be indulged in alike, by all,
Church members and non Church members.
There was also what may be called general
loose living. A child is born, its father unknown. Another is born, its mother unmarried. The responsible man, or, the unfortunate mother, or both, might be Church members. All such things were considered under
the new regime. Dear old Friendship now
became the Ecclesiastical Court House, as well
as the Church. For any of the above named
lapses, hitherto unnoticed, a member was liable at any "Quarterly Meeting" to be called to
face charges and complaints.

The general course of procedure was, by calling a church meeting. All the accused persons would be duly notified to be on hand. The meeting would be opened by singing and prayer, and then the minister, acting as the chairman, would begin at the head of the list and call case after case, according to the number to be tried. The accusation would be stated; the accused asked to plead, and make any other statement he wished in his own interest. Call for witnesses pro and con; ask the members of the Church present if they had anything to say, then, entertain a motion which would be put to the congregation. The motion might be: "not guilty;" or, "guilty of indiscretion" and reprimanded, or "set back for three months;" or, guilty, and suspended for six months, or a year, or expelled.

If the culprit showed proper "contrition," he stood a good chance to get off with a mild sentence. But if he seemed to show no signs of sorrow and regret, but rather, to show a spirit of defiance, the disposition would be to give him the "full extent of the law," and sometimes it was unwritten law, with no court of appeals.

On one occasion a married man was accused of paying so much attention to a lady other

than his wife, that it was creating a scandal.
When the case was called the accused was
asked to plead. He stated in a rather indifferent manner, that he took the lady in
question, home one rainy night under his umbrella, but, he saw no harm in that. This
savored of a direct challenge of the judgment
of the Court. "He may not be intentionally
guilty of wrong doing" said Uncle Alfred Bacon. "But he shows no signs of contrition."
This exasperated the accused, who, with considerable feeling, and with his voice at a high
pitch, shouted: "I suppose you want me to
cry like Henry Jones did, but I can't cry."
Such defiance at such a solemn and critical moment, seemed to have nonplussed the jury;
having the same effect as the "boldness of
Peter and John." After a few moments of
silence, the chairman, Elder Johnson said:
"Brer Chris, we'll let you off this time, but
hereafter, you must be more sparing in the
use of your umbrella."

This was a most excellent example set by
the unsophisticated, and really inexperienced
members of Friendship. The example is worthy of being copied by more pretentious congregations: by Churches enjoying greater advantages. So far as I have been able to keep

track of the history of the Church in question since those early days, I have reason to believe that it has in a large measure been influenced by the example set by those who were first in control.

As much cannot be said of all the Churches, which, like Friendship, was emancipated from slavery conditions. Old habits have a way of holding on tenaciously. The aftermath of slavery appeared in many different forms. The lusts of the master class that had for so many years held undisputed sway, was not to be destroyed by the wave of the hand. It was sagacious enough to "stoop to conquer," and virile enough to return after a time with "seven other spirits more wicked than himself" and make "the last state of the man worse than the first."

I have been advised of several cases where unmarried women were rearing families of mixed blood, whose fathers supported the illegitimate family, as he did his legitimate family at home: furnishing house, marketing and physician. Dr. ———— drove me by such a home in the City of ———— where I saw the innocent and well kept quadroons playing on the lawn. The father being a man of means and influence, defied public sentiment, and

held family number one in servile submission.
But his influence did not stop there: he would
have it understood that his mistress must not
be Churched, but rather must be regarded as
a leading spirit at the Church to which she
belonged, and which he gave her means to
liberally support.. If he had power enough
to enslave his own legitimate family, forcing
even the wife into unwilling silence, and besides, to so maintain himself in society as to
prevent a general protest, it is not to be won-
dered at, that the Colored Community, dependent, perilous, would also hold its peace. The
preachers and teachers of such communities,
especially in the rural districts, would be made
to understand that their presence there as
"ladies and gentlemen" would be tolerated upon the condition that they knew how to "mind
their own business." It is not difficult to see
the degrading effect that such public sentiment would have even upon the Church.

With the Church question settled and a
minister installed, we must now turn our attention to the lamentable educational needs of
the freedmen of Cecil County. Cecilton had
led off in moral reform, and must now be
depended upon to take the lead in opening a
public school, even before political matters

were sufficiently readjusted to permit of a public school under the auspices of an Educational Board. The Jane Coppin private school, and the Horace Brown Sunday School had answered their purpose, and had done well, but no time must be lost now in finding a teacher with a certificate, who can teach the grades.

Father Jones had nephew who was named for him, and was everywhere known as "Christopher Jones, Jr." His father died when he was but a child. I have often heard him say that the only recollection he had of his father was, that he once took him up in his arms, and sang: "good news, good news, the Angels brought the tidings down." He must have been quite young when his father died, to have remembered only this one thing about him. Fortunate it was for him to have come so completely as he did under the control of his wise and distinguished uncle. To this his mother readily and willingly consented, and, in rearing the lad, and in every way directing his course, the uncle was in the place of the father, and took the same interest in his brother's child that he would have taken had he been his very own. Christopher, Jr., looked more like his uncle than he did like his father; tall and slender like him, tho not as tall. In other respects too, he was like him, and principally with respect to his moral and religious character.

There was no one to write him up as the boy who never told a lie." The fact is no one who could write cared a whit whether he lied or told the truth, but all were bound to acknowledge in the end, that he was a model for the neighborhood. I once heard Alfred Hercy Price say of him: "There is no man in the county more respected than Christopher Jones. Alfred Hercy Price was a Cecilton merchant; was about the age of Christopher, and knew him from his childhood.

His lot was to knock around on the farms among the slaves and free boys of his day. He, taking the condition of his mother, was free. His widowed mother morally strong, industrious, economical, and herself under the guidance of her wonderful brother-in-law, kept a home, however humble, where the lad could come on Sundays, and holidays and receive the impressions that were destined to counter act the impressions of the daily environments and lay the foundation for his future life. He had to become a bread earner quite early in life, and was subject to the rough usage that is the common lot of the farm boy: or, that was in those days.

His uncle impressed him with the idea of being honest, industrious and economical. That he showed care for his health, his morals, and his mother. These instructions were not bestowed upon him in vain. He united with the Church when but a lad, and found an open door of useful activities for one of his bent, first as a class leader, and then as a local preacher. The older people were quick to see in him the unusual, and were not only anxious to encourage him in his aspirations, but were glad to have his services. He became the class leader of "Uncle" Abe Kennard, the hardest man in the church to please. Uncle Abe had such high opinion of him as a Christian, that he thought him quite incapable of moral delinquency. Others shared the same opinion, and the beauty of the whole thing was, they were correct.

He soon learned to save money like his uncle, though he was not destined to follow the same course in life. He was to live in a different day, when other paths would be open to him. He saved some money before the close of the war, and decided to go away from home and attend school. The Nation was so busily engaged in war between the North and South, that there was but little time to watch the Negroes and see that those in Maryland did not cross over into Deleware. And besides, it did not seem worth while to go to the trouble and expense to place the additional guards that would now be necessary for the events of the war early pointed to Emancipation. So, with the course open, Young Jones found his way to Wilmington, Del., and entered the private school of one Frisby John Cooper, who afterwards became a leading minister in the A. M. E. Church, preaching in the New Jersey and New England Conferences.

Young Jones was the first lad of our neighborhood to attend school away from home. By the time the war closed, and Cecilton, under reconstruction was planning to actually open a day school in dear old Friendship.

Christopher Jones, Jr., was "Charlie on the spot," back from a few terms of study, and ready to take the lead in the new enterprise. The few hundred dollars saved at hard work had been spent in a way to bring compound interest in more ways than one. He was to be the immediate successor of his uncle, who had guided the dependent multitudes through the darkness of the night, principally by faith, but who with the new requirements of the opening day, must hand the work over to another. And what could have brought more joy to his heart than to see his nephew, bearing his name, and fresh from his fostering care, leading to higher heights the people who for years he had carried upon his soul, and had many a time said: "O Lord how long," as he earnestly prayed that a better and brighter day would dawn.

When the time came, Father Jones was in full possession of all his faculties. He could sing and shout, and pray and rejoice with others as the glory of the new freedom broke upon them: and what a time of rejoicing it was!

Events began to follow each other with great rapidity.

1865—The Horace Brown Sunday School, with day school studies; the fall of Richmond; the coming of Bishop Wayman; the organization of an African Methodist Episcopl Church.

1866—The coming of a minister in charge; the attempt of the M. E. Chuch to hold our property; the decision of the court in our favor; the coming of Miss Sarah Christmas, our first teacher in a regular day school, and our first certificated teacher.

Our new leader, Christopher Jones, Jr., was instrumental in bringing about this glorious accomplishment.

The school was opened in January; January and February were the months of comparative leisure among farmers. The first of March was the date when hired men for the most part began the season's work. Now, all were free and all would be hired men. There would be a general rush to school, not only by boys and girls, but men and women above school age; of the latter, principally men.

Such spelling, and reading, and writing, and ciphering!!

The "First Class' was ready. The Jane Coppin private school, and the Horace Brown Sunday School had made this possible. This was a most interesting school. It was intensely "graded." From A, B, C's to the first lessons in Smith's Grammar, and the advanced class in Green's Arithmetic. Those who came, came with hunger and thirst, and applied themselves. In many instances the advancement was most remarkable. The fact is, Miss Christmas, by her own confession, afterwards had to study day and night to keep ahead of her First Class, which, by the way, was subdivided until it contained but two persons, Christopher Jones, Jr., and another one, both of whom succeeded Miss Christmas as teachers—principal and assistant—for she, after a few terms, found a position that paid her a better salary, and with pupils in higher grades.

Let it be said to the credit of Maryland, with all her faults, and she has many, that she was among the first among states to establish a public school system alike for colored and white, paying the teachers the same salaries according to grade. To-day, the City of Baltimore, the Metropolitan City of the South, is, in her school work among the colored youth, abreast of the large cities of the North and West, except, the schools are not mixed even in the higher grades, and perhaps may not be for some time to come, unless the present world war succeeds in establishing true democracy. The public school is the proper place for democracy to begin. Children playing on the streets and in the parks; newsboys selling papers, lunching and hobnobbing together think nothing and care nothing about "color" until it is injected by the satanic spirit of color prejudice by older persons.

My conversion preceded the day school by a year, having occurred in the fall of 1865.

It was conversion, genuinely so. A new birth, according to Scripture; according to nature, reason, necessity." Ye **must** be born again." These words are true. As the world swings away from this truth, it swings toward rocks and breakers. "Hiding rocks and treacherous shoals." Perhaps the world is finding this out. In most sermons, and public speeches of a more serious kind, some mention is made of the fact that unrighteousness is the real cause of the bloody conflict in which the world is engaged. Our boasted civilization, with its magic, not to say miraculous advance in the arts and sciences, has reached its height by engaging in a competitive conflict among the nations stronger and higher up, as to which can invent the most deadly weapons, and use them most effectively in the destruction of human life. The continuance of this could but result in the destruction of the human race. It is already being said that the war can only be won by man power. With the death-dealing weapons of gigantic killing power that all are using who are engaged in the conflict, it is easy to decide that those who can produce the largest number of men for the slaughter, can remain longest on the field of battle.

Is there anything higher and better than this in civilization? Yes, verily, in Christian civilization?

The world has seen great revivals of religion, and, it has seen great wars. The one meant life, and more abundantly; the other meant death, with increasing barbarity. If the conflict is not sufficient to teach the folly of trusting in human wisdom and invention, to the exclusion of Divine wisdom and guidance, then may we wonder that further chastisement will be necessary to bring back to God His prodigal world.

Saint Paul seemed never to tire referring to his conversion. "At mid-day, O, King, a light from heaven above the brightness of the sun." That is the brief record of what actually happened. That light "from heaven" blinded his natural eyes, but most unmistakably cleared his spiritual vision and understanding, so that, he never again "conferred with flesh and blood." It is not given to all men who are converted, to have such a sudden and marvelous physical demonstration of a spiritual change, but the "light from heaven" is quite real to every truly awakened soul;

and they are legion who bear testimony, not alone in words, but more so in their lives, to the reality of the spiritual birth.

My conversion in the days of my youth was the first satisfying evidence to an anxious mother, that she had not hoped and prayed in vain: that "Santa Claus" had not mocked her.

The fact that the Christmas baby, the very youngest member of the "first class" stood by odds, and without challenge at its head, was sufficient to cause a mother of prayer and faith to treasure in her heart, and regard with full value those intellectual signs of promise. But even precocity itself is not a sufficient evidence that the ruling passion will be spiritual.

My conversion made me available for service in the church as well as in the school room. So soon as I finished my "six months on probation" I was elected superintendent of the Sunday school, and with this responsibility began my study of the Scriptures in earnest. I always had a desire to do well whatever I undertook, even if it was ploughing a field or marking out corn rows. I had the reputation of running rows so straight that the most critical examination could not discover a crook in them.

But at last there had come to me a responsibility that I was far from being equal to. But,
it was a blessing in disguise. It compelled
study, research, prayer, and constant application to the things in the line of particular
duty, "Where there is a will there is a way."
says the old adage, which experience has more
or less verified.

The International system of lessons was not
then in vogue. There were no topics, titles,
outlines, golden texts, reference words and
Scriptural references to guide and assist the
student and teacher. There was no such thing
as "primary department" and graded classes
further along. It was just the cold, hard,
"dry" study of the Bible. There were no lesson helps and teachers' meetings. Perhaps it
was well enough for us to begin that way. We
committed to memory a great deal of Scripture, and such a course is of inestimable
value to the Bible student. The ability to
quote the Scripture correctly is of great advantage to the preacher and Sunday school
teacher, and it is to be feared that the easier
methods of "lesson helps" and commentaries
have "helped" to the detriment of individual
growth. This is not to pronounce against
helps to the study of the Scriptures, but care

should be taken, that they do not largely take the place of the Scriptures. But, with all the handicap, and conscious inability, it was a great thing for a lad to actually be the accredited superintendent of Sunday school at Friendship, at this glorious period, when old things had passed away and all things had become new. At a period when leadership was decisive and unquestionable. When to have the confidence of the community was to have its unstinted support.

Two ministers came to us as supplies, namely, I. J. Pindle and Stephen P. Bayard, but the first regular preacher to come and remain was William H. Hopkins. He was a man of irreproachable character, and easily in the lead of his people intellectually. In fact, he was a most remarkable man for his day. He was born at Easton, on the famous Eastern Shore of Maryland, and is one of the many bright lights who is but little known in history. He was of unmixed African blood, with hair perfectly white, and a face that would suggest a man much younger than he evidently was. His step was quick and firm, and he could make the round of his circuit on foot, a distance of fourteen miles, without showing signs of fatigue. He had a clear, ringing

voice, and was above the average as a preacher. He had a high opinion of himself as a man
and a gentleman, and never showed the cring-
ing spirit in any presence. He was evidently
one of the free born men whose spirit had
never been broken by the cruel lash of the
slave driver. He had lofty ideals, and delighted to bring to his work the most representative men of the day. This was very fortunate for the church he served at the time
of his administration. The people of Cecilton
had never seen an educated colored man,
technically speaking, nor had they ever seen
white men who believed in their educational
advancement. If there were any such persons around they did not, in the face of prevailing public sentiment, express an opinion
loud enough to be heard.

Reverend Hopkins planned to bring in certain men whom he hoped would convince the
young people that a bright future was possible for them, and that it was well worth
while to strive for it.

The first one to come upon the scene to instruct and inspire, was the Rev. James F. Sisson, a New England Yankee, of unmixed Cau-
casian blood. He was a regularly ordained
traveling preacher in the A. M. E. Church. A

standing and outspoken protest against color prejudice and proscription in any and every form. He could say "brother" and "sister" and mean it. He was cultured, refined and an earnest, untiring worker.

His field of operation had been entirely in the East, where the voice of the abolitionist was accustomed to ring out, even when there was a plenty of opposition to it. Where Garrison and Philips, and Greeley, and Thaddeus Stevens, Lucretia Mott, William H. Furness, Robert Purvis, Frederick Douglass and such immortal souls had made it safe for an honest man to honestly express an honest opinion.

Reverend Hopkins wished that his parishioners might hear some of that free and wholesome speech that would incline them to straighten up, and feel like men. And so, upon a day appointed, Brother Sisson made his appearance in Friendship. He preached at the morning service and was announced to address the children and young people especially in the afternoon.

By some means, I know not how, it became known in town that a "white man was at the 'nigger' church calling the 'niggers' brother and sister."

Promptly at the appointed afternoon hour
Reverend Sisson was at his post; but, as
promptly, stationed at one of the side windows, was a number of the lowest, meanest,
and most ignorant whites that the town afforded. They were there to hear for themselves what was said, and to prove that though
Richmond had fallen, and Lee had surrendered, every nook and corner of the United
States had not been brought into immediate
subjection, and that Cecilton was one of the
places not subdued.

Reverend Sisson, nothing daunted by their
presence, began his address. He referred
briefly to the origin of the A. M. E. Church,
and stated that it was its purpose and mission
to demonstrate to the world that the colored
man was susceptible of the same development,
morally, intellectually and otherwise, that any
other race variety was." "That's a lie,"
promptly rang out from the leader of the mob.

The speaker, paying no attention to the insult, and interruption, continued to speak of
the Church, its progress under the most serious difficulties. Its Book Concern in Philadelphia; its weekly periodical, the Christian
Recorder; its Wilberforce College in Ohio, recently acquired, and its eight full-fledged

Bishops, namely, Bishops Allen, Morris, Brown, Waters, Quinn, Nazrey, Payne, Wayman and Campbell.

This was indeed a flood of light thrown upon a question concerning which every one present knew but little or nothing except the speaker himself and the minister in charge; and it was more than the outside mob could consent to listen to longer. The disturbance that followed broke up the meeting completely, and it was with much difficulty that Reverend Sisson was rushed to a place of safety, while the frightened congregation scattered in different directions. No one was seriously hurt thanks to good fortune, and poor leadership by the mob.

In a round-about way, Reverend Sisson was piloted away from the place and sent to Chesapeake City, thence to Baltimore, where he made complaint at the Freedmen's Bureau. Nothing came of the case, however, except the mob never troubled any one else who came among us, and this was a warning to our people to prepare for self-protection, which some were quick to do, while others, fearful of a recurrence, absented themselves for a time from public gatherings.

The next person of distinction to visit us was Mr. George C. Cook, of Baltimore, a lecturer, who represented a newspaper called *The True Communicator*. It was published at Douglass Institute, No. 11 Lexington Street, Baltimore, Md. His coming was heralded as the coming of an educated colored man, and the first of his class to visit Cecilton. We were all somewhat shy of him, but some one must come forward, shoulder the cross, and play the host for our distinguished visitor. He stopped at my father's house, and I was mother's "best man" to do the entertaining.

I can remember but one idea advanced by him, and that was concerning the literature of Greece. But whether we understood him well or not, or remembered much or little of what he said, we felt pleased to have a Negro scholar among us, and many of us subscribed to his paper. It was something quite new to see us crowd into the little post office on Saturdays, after "Mr. Slaughter" had come with the mail, getting into line with others and march up to the window for our weekly paper. During all the years of the past but one paper came to that town for a colored man, namely Father Jones, and that came in the name of Henry Hays, the school teacher.

Another distinguished visitor to Cecilton was Rev. W. D. W. Schureman, the most popular preacher of his day and generation in our Church. Reverend Hopkins was determined that we should from time to time get to see a fair sample of what the race and Church had produced, and thereby strengthen our confidence in the race, and increase our love for the Church. We had been shut up all our lives in our narrow little neck, and all else was measured by it. With us, the richest man was "the richest man in Sassafras Neck." The fastest horse was "the fastest horse in Sassafras Neck." When the "bully" could "lick any man," it was "any man in Sassafras Neck." What a wonderful Neck, ours! The nearest railroad was nine miles away, at Middletown, Del., and the nearest city was Wilmington, Del., thirty miles away. It would be some time before we could pick ourselves up and visit the great world on the outside; and so, the Hopkins plan was to, little by little, bring the world to us. A man, connected with a large family of aunts, uncles, cousins, etc., got married, left his home and settled down elsewhere. News came one day that he had died and would be buried at his new home. All the relatives, near and distant, wished very much to look once more into his face. But it would cost considerable for any one to go, and much more for all to go. So some one suggested the idea of bringing the corpse back home, and let all get a look, then send it on for burial.

All arrangements were made for the preacher to come, and a stand was erected in front of the church, out in the grove. It was summer time, with nature at her best, and the weather man in his happiest mood. Through the tall oak trees of the grove a gentle wind passed; just enough to fan the leaves to sufficient motion to cause one to "hear the sound thereof." The sun might do his best at high noon, but those old sentinels stood as umbrellas to afford shade for the multitudes below. Sassafras Neck was again the proud host of all the Necks below.

James Ferrel was early on hand, ready and willing to tell the time to any one, for this gave him a chance to exhibit his last acquisition in the way of a timekeeper, and explain what make it was. "Mose" Cain, "once in grace, and always out," could be depended upon to be present on such an occasion. Of course, all the old regulars were there, and on time, to witness all that took place, and take a real spiritual part in all the preliminary services, and to have a comfortable place from which to listen to the preaching.

"And I saw, as it were, a sea of glass, mingled with fire," exclaimed the preacher. Revelation 15:2.

"Look away to yonder mountain: a stream of water silently wends its way down the rugged slope until it reaches the vale below. Then taking its course through the valley, it widens and deepens as it goes rushing toward the sea." Then, with figurative language, quite worthy of the book from which he took his text, the great preacher held his audience spellbound, having them as completely at his command as had the wind the leaves of the trees above us. For a long time after that, at any fireside could be heard some mention of "Schormon," and "the sea of glass all mingled with fire."

It was not unusual to hear men take their text from the Revelation, and create an expectation for something mysterious and unusual. But, as a rule, the mystery did not go beyond the reading of the text, and one could often hear the remark: "He didn't do nothin' with it." Not so with "Schormon." It seemed that every one went away satisfied that he had abundantly sustained the reputation given him by Pastor Hopkins. It was "a day long to be remembered." There were many whites around, but they were as completely under the spell of the magic orator as were the simple-hearted colored auditors. "Where did he come from" was the prevalent question. To this Pastor Hopkins, with a twinkle of the eye, and a cunning smile all his own, would reply: "We have a plenty more like him."

One of the things connected with the history of our people, not generally known or considered, and what seems mysterious even to those who consider it, is the fact that in 1866, one year after the Surrender, the A. M. E. Church was fifty years old in its organic form, and seventy-nine years old counting from the date, 1787, when the revolt against segregation at St. George took place. Just how this handful of people, without social, political and civil prestige; poor and unlearned, and hemmed in from every side by slavery, and the spirit and influence of slavery, could organize and maintain itself so long and so well, is, indeed, a mystery. One would not imagine, until his attention is called to the fact, that at the dawn of freedom, there was a regularly organized religious denomination; with Bishops, a Book Repository, a weekly newspaper, hymn book and discipline and a church school. With seven annual conferences operating in different states, as follows: the New England, New York, Pennsylvania, Maryland, Ohio, Indiana and Missouri.

The Twelfth General Conference met in Philadelphia—birthplace of the Church—in 1864, and the table of statistics, as printed in the minutes, shows the following: Members and probationers, 50,000; traveling preachers, 500; local preachers, 2000; property valued at $2,000,000; number of churches, 1600; a number of school-houses and one university, namely, Wilberforce, at—near—Zenia, Ohio.

Another fact not generally known, and one that the Denomination should ever have full credit for, is, that from the very beginning, there was no discrimination in membership, on account of color; and, from the very beginning there were white persons connected in some way with the Church—members, ministers, professors. This, I think, was largely due to Bishop D. A. Payne, whose influence had much to do with shaping the policy of the Church. He bitterly opposed any tendency to reject, or make it unpleasant for persons of other race varieties who came among us. He denounced it as being unchristian, and just as sinful for colored persons to discriminate against whites, as for whites to discriminate against colored. Many of our people, feeling the sting of discrimination, stood ready to make it uncomfortable for any white person attending our services. But this spirit would be promptly rebuked by the leaders, and in every way discouraged, as it deserved to have been.

On account of the strong abolition spirit prevalent at the time the Church was organized, there were many who had conscientious scruples about receiving the Holy Communion in a Church that rejected the Brotherhood. The sentiment against so-called "social equality" kept many from taking an independent stand, and also accounts for many who were skeptical, and avoided the church altogether. But there were some, who, in the face of ostracism, satisfied their consciences and united with the Church, whose doors were open to all. This accounts for James F. Sisson in our ministry in the early sixties, and for a large number who followed his example. To be sure, the proportion is small compared with the entire membership; it is only one here and there. But the principle remains the same. They can join if they wish, and it may be that when the

Christian Church becomes Christianized, color will be relegated and Christ exalted.

Following the Surrender, a number of celebrations were held in the big grove. These were intended to celebrate the great event, the Emancipation. Our Sunday school superintendent, now a recognized leader among the young people, was the promoter of these gatherings. It was upon such an occasion that a brass band was first heard in Cecilton. The services of the Mount Vernon Cornet Band of Wilmington, Del., of which James A. Harding was leader, were secured. The author of "Sherman's March Through Georgia" sings of how the turkeys gobbled when they heard the music sound. I think such a characterization would be quite applicable in describing the impression made upon man, and beast, and fowls, when, one morning, the quiet of Cecilton was disturbed for the first time by a real brass band, with uniformed men, playing upon the various pieces that compose a full band.

Cecilton is but a cross-roads. So the band, starting at the grove, would approach the town from the south, and proceed north as far as the stately residence of "Dr. Roberts," our dear old Dr. Roberts! We thought we could not get well of a spell of sickness until we had taken a few of his big, brown, bitter pills.

The procession would then counter-march to the center of the town, right at the cross-roads, and turning east, around the Cruik-shank store, proceed as far as Back Street gate. Returning, go west to Sanders Town, then, south on a bee-line to the stand in front of the church.

No one among us could pass upon the merits or demerits of the music. No one could detect a discord if any were made. It sounded mighty good to us, and as far as the winds wafted it to distant fields, men, women and children would hasten to town to witness the great event. Peter S. Blake, afterwards one of my music teachers, played in the band.

On one of these occasions the orator was Frisby John Cooper. Of course his services had been secured through the efforts of his pupil, Christopher Jones, Jr. He was anxious for Cecilton to see and hear the man who had first directed him in a literary pursuit, and the speaker was evidently as anxious to see the home of the tall young countryman who had, even while the war was yet in progress, come to him from the country of Frederick Douglass, seeking knowledge.

Reverend Cooper was a precise, deliberate speaker. With ringing accent he would stand out every vowel, and never neglect the final consonant. He stood about five feet ten. Head bald and shining through the middle. Face ebony black. Teeth like rows of ivory. A piercing eye, and his face wearing a smile of confidence. He "knew his piece" and could speak it. He used only notes, and looking his auditors squarely in the eye, would fairly charm them. His magnetic face would secure for him attention, and his arguments were always convincing.

Upon another celebration occasion we had, as orator of the day, exactly the counterpart of Frisby J. Copper, namely, William Howard Day, the matchless orator, who never used a scrap of paper, not even to verify historical facts and dates; he, himself, being a veritable cyclopaedia of facts. He was a mulatto; tall, slender, agile. In style, very much like James G. Blaine. His hair, as black as a coal, fell in ringlets upon his shoulders. In grace of movement, a veritable Chesterfield. As I remember it now, he was an Oberlin man. This was the first American college of note to accept colored students. Well, Howard Day, "gained the day" that day. We had moved the speaker's stand from its accustomed place in front of Friendship, back of the grove, to a spot in front of the grove, not far from the "Brick Church." This, I think was partly a bid for the white population and partly a suggestion that we were no longer obliged to stay behind the wood, neither to hide our ignorance, nor to avoid friction. The old Sisson riot had become a thing of the past, and all the men who came to speak for and represent the race were either unmistakably "Colored," like Wayman and Cooper, or who like Howard Day, were classed as such.

Those celebrations accomplished two or three worthy objects: they brought to one of the dark corners of the earth men who represented the higher and better element of our people, a much-needed lesson for both colored and white to learn.

Then, it brought harmoniously together the "two races," and led to a better understanding. When Howard Day finished his speech, I went to Dr. Harry Crookshanks, who had been an attentive listener through the whole of the service, and said: "How do you like him." I was not quite prepared for the answer. Had not thought of it in that light. The doctor said: "He is very fine, but he is not a fair representative of the colored people."

Another thing accomplished by those celebrations was, we collected money with which to build our new church. Our people just from slavery, had not much to give, and must needs be trained to give liberally of what little they had. Christopher Jones, Sr., led off with a subscription of twenty-five dollars, a "monstrous" large sum to us. Christopher Jones, Jr., and James Martemore Chaney—"Mart Chanye"—followed with a like amount. But all the rest came in much smaller amounts. Wages were low. When James C. White, superintendent of the Reybold's Island—formerly Knight's Island—peach farm, announced that he would give "five levies a day"—sixty-two and one-half cents, for picking peaches, men and women alike rushed to the orchard farm "down the Island" to share the "big wages!" I am advised now that, August, 1918, Cecil County farmers are offering from two dollars to two-fifty per day for farm laborers, and that it is difficult to secure enough even at those figures.

"Father Jones," about whom much has been said, and about whom too much cannot be said, had quite a lot of wood corded up in "Price's

Woods," near Cecilton, when the recruiting officers came there. He had always "worked the rabbit foot" on the white folks and got on with them. When some ignorant and jealous Negro would brand him as being an "ole dimmecrat," he never took the trouble to explain. So, when the soldiers at the recruiting office, under Lieutenant Brown, got short of wood, they helped themselves from the cords of the "Negro Democrat."

He made no protest, and no explanation. I imagine he rather rejoiced that he was fortunate enough to have wood to keep the soldiers warm, and cook the food of the men who had come to help open the door for freedom.

On March 5th, 1869, President U. S. Grant appointed John A. J. Creswell, of Port Deposit, Md., Postmaster General. This was Father Jones' opportunity. He had patiently waited for six years, saying nothing about the loss of his wood. Now, a Marylander is in the Cabinet, and through him Father Jones made an appeal for damages, which he recovered. I do not know the amount he recovered, but he doubtless "received his own with usury."

It was to him a sore trial to go day by day and year by year under the implication, and sometimes under the definite charge that politically

he held with the slave-holding class, as against
the best interests of his people, that he might
himself be materially benefitted. He had stood
for years as the very embodiment of honor,
in all that an honorable life can stand for. No
person, colored or white, had ever questioned
his right to this rare distinction. But this very
fact now made his position among the people a
peculiar one. His own people expected him to
feel and act in their interest to the fullest extent that it was possible for him to do so;
while the master class felt that he could be
depended upon to say nothing and do nothing
that could be at all interpreted as being insur-
rectional. He had actually refused to learn to
write, lest he might be accused of writing
"passes" for slaves. On the other hand, the
slaves, bearing their heavy burdens, expected
him to sympathize with them, and stand ready,
at any time, to help them if it were possible
to do so. But he could be of the greatest service to them by standing aloof from all matters
of controversy between the abolitionists and
the pro-slavery people. He had no vote, and
therefore was not forced to show his hand at
the polls. When the war broke out, however
much he was in sympathy with the Union
forces and the cause of freedom, it was not the

time to speak out. When the recruiting officers came enlisting colored men for the service, it was thought by many that he should
then declare himself; hob-nob about the recruiting office, and assist in getting men to enlist. But he felt differently and still stood
aloof. It was then that some one whispered
to Lieutenant Brown and his men that Cecilton enjoyed the novelty of having a Negro
Democrat. That he could possess his soul in
patience under circumstances most trying was
one of the best evidences of his ability to be
a true leader among his people. But the time
came at last when he could speak out, and
speak out he did. He left no room for doubt
as to what had been his true attitude during
all the long years of the past. He could then
explain why he took the position of a neutral.
Then every one could see the wisdom of his
course.

There was one man among the whites who
was always regarded as being in sympathy
with the abolition cause, namely, Thomas
Jones, whose farm was adjoining the village
of Cecilton, and strange to say, he was himself a slave-holder on a small scale, the size
of which made no difference in its moral as-
pect. The first celebration and parade of the

colored people after the Surrender proceeded
to his home. There were a few other Republicans in the village, but none of them were
aggressive. Some of them secretly aided in
Underground Railroad work: Isaac Slaughter,
for instance, the mail-stage driver.

The next minister appointed to Friendship
was Rev. William M. Johnson. Bishop Wayman, who had a habit of nick-naming, called
him "Greenland Johnson." He came to us from
the New York Conference. He was not the
equal in scholarship of Pastor Hopkins, but,
like him, he was progressive, and unlike him,
could gather about him the young people, inspire them with confidence in themselves, and
set them at work along new lines.

I always had a natural gift for "pitching
tunes," and singing; a sort of maternal in-
heritance. After uniting with the church, the
older people soon learned to depend upon me
to direct the singing. They had much trouble
with the metres, and with pitch. Once started,
off they could go on all right, but the trouble
was getting started. To me it was quite natural, even before I took any lessons in vocal
music. I would pitch the common, long and
short metres in familiar tunes, and actually
originate tunes for some of the so-called par-

ticular metres. But I was conscious all the time that these home-made tunes were but makeshifts, and I only awaited an opportunity to take up the study of vocal music, and prepare myself to do scientifically and correctly the work that I was forced to do by guess.

The first music book that I remember ever to have seen, with lines and spaces, and dots and stems, and sharps and flats, and naturals, and the usual distribution of musical terms, indicating movement, regulation of the voice, and the like, was indeed a mystery to me. The notes, scattered all about over the lines and spaces, and above and below, seemed unintelligible. But there came to Cecilton a music teacher, Quimby by name, and opened a singing school for the white people. I stole alongside of the school house where I could see them, being in the light, and at the same time, being myself outside in the darkness, would not be observed. All I could hear was do, do; re, re: mi, mi: fa, fa, etc. At the end of an exercise Professor Quimby came to some girls who sat near the window into which I was clandestinely peeping, and said they had not made certain notes correctly, and, first going over them himself he had them to follow. His explanation to them was magical to me. It

seemed perfectly cléar, then, that however
they looked to me, those notes were methodi-
cally placed on those lines and spaces and
could be learned. I went away from that window with an inspiration, and a resolve, acting upon which I never ceased my efforts until
I stood Quimby like, directing a chorus made
up of our young people, who, with books in
hand, were singing by note.

The old people were not anxious to see radi-
cal innovations introduced in religious worship. Some of them doubtless would not hesitate to adopt the sentiments expressed in the
lines:

> "They've got a chorister and choir
> Against my voice and vote;
> For it was never my desire
> To serve the Lord by note."

But old Greenland was on hand to tell the
young people to go ahead, and what was more,
to go with them. He seemed to have happened there for such a time.

Uncle Abe Kennard would characterize as:
"hifallutin grammer," anything interjected in
worship that was outside of the ordinary, and
Uncle James Sisco stood ready to lambaste
any member of his class who was reported as

becoming too worldly. But Pastor Johnson was on hand to see to it that no reactionary threw any stumbling blocks in the way of his progressive young set, so long as "L. J." was leading them. After years had passed, and his "L. J." was pastor of Bethel Church, Baltimore, he seemed to take especial pride in saying: "I found that boy in the bushes, but look at him now." All credit and all honor to "Pap Johnson" as we boys called him, for giving the needed word of encouragement at the right time. All credit and all honor to Uncle James and Uncle Abe for timely counsel at the period of our religious career when it was most needed. All credit and all honor to Pastor Hopkins, who set himself the task of bringing among us men to create confidence and to inspire with hope. There were a few of the older people who were quite prepared for the new conditions. They were veritable progressives. They stood all right on the fundamentals. They believed in "sound conversion," and upright living, but they were not afraid to put "new wine in new bottles." They had been deprived of literary training, of which they were conscious, but they had a high degree of intelligence and rejoiced that they had lived to see the day when their children, the young people, had a chance to prepare themselves for service upon a higher intellectual plane. "Uncle" Alfred Bacon, the step-father of Christopher Jones, Jr., was among the foremost of this class.

The coming of the day school, and the singing school were timely and valuable moral and intellectual helps among a people hitherto deprived of uplifting influences. Under the old regime, the morals and intellect of the colored youth were not at all taken into account. He was allowed "to get religion;" even encouraged so to do. But just think of religion separated from morality! Stealing was not complained of so long as you did not steal from your master. It was all right to get drunk if you were sober in due time to go to work in the morning, and do your full task. Nothing was thought of being the father or mother of an illegitimate child. The multiplication of children, like the multiplication of cattle, was of material advantage to the master, and he did not permit the injection of any moral code for his slaves that would make against his material interest.

The ministers, the proper religious teachers, were, like all others, under the dominating influence of the slave-holding oligarchy, with

the exception of here and there a heroic one,
who like Elijah, was willing to stand alone.

Keep a people thus, in moral and intellectual darkness for a period of two hundred and
fifty years, and what could be expected of
them but ignorance and moral deficiency. The
very fact, that, in spite of such environment,
there were many with highly developed intel-
lects, and many possessing moral strength to
an amazing degree, is an argument in favor of
the unity of the human race, and the moral
nature and moral power of God. As to intellect, Frederick Douglass, Benjamin Banneker
and Philis Wheatley are well-known examples
and these are not all. As to morals, the world
will never know of the heroes and heroines;
heroines especially. Their history is unwritten; largely unknown because tradition has
failed to take cognizance of most cases, and
besides, nearly all who knew of them, have
passed away, and with them the knowledge
is buried. Think of an enraged master, standing with a red hot poker, giving a defenseless
slave girl, who had dared to resist and fight
him, her choice between submitting, or under-
going hellish tortures that cannot be named.
Mrs. Jane Evans related a case of the kind
about which she had personal knowledge. Mrs.

Evans was a woman whose veracity was above question, and for such a woman to invent a fabrication, too horrible for the most gigantic imagination, is unthinkable. The case did not relate to our informant, and hence there was no attempt to exalt one's own virtues. This is not written in the book of martyrs. Slaves had no such biographers. Even the school books in our American courses of study are silent upon any kind of heroic or brave deeds performed by the people of African descent. This, I think, is a sufficient apology for calling up such unpleasant memories. Our people are not yet out of the wilderness of proscription and prejudice. Civil, political and economic rights, privileges and opportunities are yet denied or given grudgingly and of necessity. It is well, therefore, even at this late day, to point out some worthy deeds of valor and sacrifice on the part of those who had naught else of value to bequeath to posterity.

History abounds with chapters, even volumes of valor, heroism and noble achievemnt on the part of those in whose interest the history is written, and for the inspiration of their posterity.

Unless we, as a people, do some writing of a historical nature, we may but expect that

much that would be inspiring and educative
to our youth, will be buried in the past, while
much that is unfavorable, and hence depress-
ing, will be exhibited as true history.   Much
there is, indeed, in the history of a century,
and of a people that is anything but complimentary. This is true to a greater or lesser
extent of any people. The Bible itself speaks
in no uncertain voice of the sins and weak-
nesses of Bible characters. But this is only one
side of the question, the other side is also
given, and all history, to be faithful and true,
will bring out both sides. No one can
charge that the sins and shortcomings of
our people have not been exhibited to the
world and are still, and constantly being put
on exhibition in many ways; even by themselves. The vicious and ignorant among us
are ever a source of comment and unfavorable
discussion.   The recent migration of multitudes from one portion of the country to another will carry its quota of good and bad,
and introduce new problems. The "Clansman"
has gone ahead with its story of slander and
misrepresentation and not altogether without
making the impression that was originally intended by the author and his sympathizers.

Let us hope that from time to time scraps

of history may come to light that will show
that "Uncle Tom's Cabin" may be reproduced
again and again, not alone in mythical, but
in real living historical characters; and not
only upon the famous Eastern Shore of Maryland, but in every portions of the country where
our people lived and moved and had their
being. Where, with unrequited toil, without
the inspiration of hope except as it is found in
blind faith, unsupported by enlightned reason,
for two hundred and forty years the African
in America adjusted himself to his condition,
sang and prayed and danced as he toiled patiently on; accepted the religion of his master, even without seeing it truly exemplified
by those who professed it, and waited for the
dawning of a day, either in time or eternity,
when "every day would be Sunday," into the
rest and joy of which even the poor, dejected
slave would be brought.

Such walking "by faith and not by sight,"
and that, too, by a faith that was largley in-
stinctive, is a unique chapter in the world's
history that is unwritten, unwriteable, and
largely unknown.

CHAPTER V.

Farewell to Cecilton

In his "Departure of Hiawatha," Longfellow sings thus, in part:

"From his place rose Hiawatha,
Bade farewell to old Nokomis,
Spake in whispers, spake in this wise,
Do not wake the guests that slumbered,
I am going, O Nokomis
On a long and distant journey
To the portals of the Sunset,
To the regions of the home-wind,
Of the northwest wind Keewaydin.
But these guests I leave behind me,
In your watch and ward I leave them;
See that never harm comes near them;
See that never fear molests them;
Never danger or suspicion,
Never want of food or shelter,
In the lodge of Hiawatha,
Forth into the village went he,

(172)

Bade farewell to all the young men;
Spake persuading, spake on this wise:
I am going, O my people,
On a long and distant journey,
Many moons and many winters,
Will have come and will have vanished,
Ere I come again to see you."

There comes a time when the birdling must leave the old nest, prove his wings, and enter upon a new and independent life. If it is an eagle, his vision goes to the far away mountains, to the exploration of which his eagle instinct suggests that he has a perfect right to aspire. There are souls that cannot become satisfied with things ordinary: that cannot become inured to cage life, or limited environments. There are eagle-like souls with broad vision, that see far away mountains, and long to discover what is yet beyond. They are not content to mark the time of their immediate surroundings, watching the smoke from the old family chimney, with a "come day go day" satisfaction, that is without the impulse that seeks new avenues of activity.

Here-in lay the mistake of slavery, and here-in slumbered its downfall.

"Under Mount Etna, he lies.
'Tis slumber: it is not death.
For often he strives to arise,
And above him the lurid skies
Are filled with his fiery breath.
The mountains are rolled on his head;
The crags are piled on his breast:
But, the sighs of his wild unrest,
Tho smothered and half suppressed
Are heard: and he is not dead."

The runaway slave by this act protested against oppression and suppression in but a milder form than the insurrection of "Nat" Turner. Much of unwritten history consists of daring deeds on the part of slaves, women and men, for their freedom, or the protection of virtue. Some of this has been purposely suppressed, and some did not come to be generally known simply because there was no scribe to chronicle it.

It is reasonable to suppose that all men who are at least normal mentally and physically prefer freedom to bondage. Not only freedom of the body to go and come at will, but freedom of the mind also, to expand, improve, and acquire a knowledge of the things with which one comes into daily contact. But the laws and customs of oppression, the crime in the eyes of the master class of anything like self-assertiveness or independence on the part of the enslaved, and its sure and sanguinary punishment such as was necessary to sustain the slave system, took all the heart and hope out of the majority of the slaves and caused them to become content in a way, with their lot. In this state of lethargic contentment, the spirit of aspiration with which nature had endowed them would depart, and with this result, slavery had accomplished its supreme object. Only from the minority then, would come the insuppressible ones, and these kept alive the fire of hope.

When freedom came, there was a large field of usefulness open to those who had in spite of their enviroments forced ahead a pace, and become the natural leaders. They were in the church, in the school, and in social and civic life generally. And there was a strong inducement to remain at home, either from a desire to be of service to the less fortunate, or from the fact, that such service, being in great demand, was liberally rewarded. In many instances the forward ones took all sorts of advantage of the backward ones; preyed upon their ignorance and credulity, and spoiled them of their first fruits of freedom.

My own position at home was rather peculiar, or, peculiarly in favor of my remaining. Besides being free born, I had the inspiration and guidance of a most remarkable mother, spoken of elsewhere in these pages. Even before the surrender, tho a youth, I was regarded as a sort of oracle by my poor benighted people, among whom I was facile princeps. I was their scribe, accountant and confidential advisor. Sunday School teacher, and chief chorister in both Sunday School and church, and finally, after two terms of tutelage under our first day school teacher Miss Christmas, elsewhere spoken of, I became day school teacher.

But conscious of my limitations, and with a burning desire to pursue my studies, and by contact with men and women of mind, character and learning, prepare my self for the highest and best purpose of life, no temporary advantages however enticing could induce me to remain at home. Abraham like, to me came the call of conscience and desire so strong as to be irresistable. And Abraham like, no specific direction was given. The impulse said go. Break away from filial and fraternal ties and obligations. Be not content to follow lines of least resistance, nor be satisfied with small accomplishments under meagre opportunities, but launch out into the deep, sink or swim.

The day came, February 15, 1869. Momentous day! My friend C. J. Hall and I, had talked the matter over again and again and at last resolved upon a course of action. We had both saved some money as a necessary preparation for such an adventure. It was the custom of those who were frugal and industrious to prepare for winter by laying aside in summer. January and February were the leisure months, and we selected this as the most suitable time for leaving home. With the opening spring came the temptation to put off going for another season, and so we determined that when the daffodil made its appearance again, and "the voice of the turtle" was heard, proclaiming the return of spring, we would be found in a different clime.

We decided to go to Philadelphia, and cast our lot among the quiet Quakers, instead of going to New York about which we had heard so much both good and evil. Then again, we had a friend in Philadelphia, a fellow countryman, who, through correspondence, spoke well of the place, and of the opportunities for a young man of grit and purpose. We requested him to secure us a suitable boarding place, and name the day when we should report.

As we did not consider ourselves paupers, and our season of leisure had not passed, we resolved to enjoy a little sight seeing before settling down to serious life. Our sight seeing need not be of an expensive kind, for this, being the largest city that we had ever seen, everything would be new and interesting. One thing we firmly and definitely decided upon, and that was to live the simple and safe life that we were accustomed to, and not seek to be initiated into the "mystic" ways of city life before our "beard grew out."

We found our way to church, Mother Bethel, on the first Sunday in town, and greatly enjoyed the services, they being so different from what we had witnessed all our lives at dear old Friendship. My first really amusing, tho very embarrasing city experience, was on this wise. The daughter of the lady with whom we boarded, invited me to accompany her to the family church on one Sunday evening. It was "Big Wesley." I had never attended that church before. "Big Wesley" was a rival of "Big Bethel" and was just around the corner from it, Bethel being on 6th St., above Lombard, and Wesley being on Lombard St., below 6th. The custom then in both city and country, was, for men to sit on one side of the church, and women on the other. So according to this custom I had to separate from my company upon entering the church. The church was well filled when we arrived, and we decided to go to the gallery, the lady taking one side and I the other. It was revival season, and after the sermon, a long one, the "prayer meeting" began. We did not think to decide upon a time to come out if the meeting should prove to be unusually long, so, there was nothing to do but to wait until the close, and then take chances on finding each other when the crowd came out. In perfect country like innocence, when I became tired out and thirsty in that big, overcrowded, over heated, and poorly ventilated church, I decided to go out and get some fresh air, and a drink of water from the hydrant in the church yard. Well, I went out. The usher at the door was polite and obliging. He was even anxious to get as many out as possible but was not permitting any one to come in. After I had slaked my thirst, and was not only cooled off, but, was cold, as it was near zero weather, I returned to the door, but only to witness the sad experience of the foolish virgins. When at last the meeting closed and

the crowd began to press out the two open
doors, I might have been about as successful
at looking for a needle in a hay stack, as I
was looking for the lady whom I had escorted.
When I arrived home late, and alone, apologiz-
ed to Miss McRay, went to my room, and related my experience to my friend C. J., he
fairly cracked his sides with his characteristic
laugh when much amused, and I think rather
enjoyed the fact that I got well paid for my
gallantry, and for not inviting him to accompany us. It is needless to say that the lesson
was so well learned that it did not have to be
repeated.

Well, here is Philadelphia! great big Philadelphia! What will we do with it? Perhaps
a far more important question is, what will
Philadelphia do with us? "Uncle" David
Brown who reached four score years, and went
beyond, came to Philadelphia from the country before the war. He was a lad in his teens.
He was fortunate enough to get a job right
away in the "Health and Vital Statistics" Department. His business was to sweep around,
keep fires, and do errands. Feeling the need
of a Savior to keep him from the evils of his
new and attractive home, he went into the
cellar of the Department, and there in the

quiet of the night, gave himself to Him who
alone can save. He never lost his job nor his
religion. He was promoted to confidential
messenger, and entrusted with keys, and
money to any amount. After he had been
in the service for fifty years and more, he was
known to all the officials, and all who came and
went, as "Uncle David." During the last years
of his life, he was relieved from specific duties
but kept on his wages. He would report to
the "City Hall" when he felt well enough, and
otherwise disposed to do so, and to make him
feel like he was still of importance about the
place, would occasionally be sent with large
sums of money to the bank. He was a class
leader in Bethel church where he had held
membership from the time he decided in the
cellar to be a christian. The church is a great
protection to a young man in a city. Anywhere
for that matter, but especially where there are
so many things to attract and allure.

My greatest desire was to get an education.
I had already a good start, but only a start.
It is true I had spent more days in school
than had my fellow countryman Fred, Douglass when he took the platform as a public
speaker, but, "on this hangs a tale." The
school house is a means to an end. The end,

is an education. The school house is the principal means, but not the only means.

Pestalozzi the great Swiss educator, Abraham Lincoln, to whose wisdom and statesmanship America and the world delights to pay tribute, and Frederick Douglass, second to none in the history of the men of his day, are illustrious examples of what can be accomplished by persistent study and application. A person may go to school and yet not study much.. May go through the world yet see but little: may come in contact with many persons and things, yet test nothing: or, may even prove many things, and yet hold fast to none: may begin, and make some progress in many branches of learning, without becoming perfect in any. How often do we hear the cry: "I did not have a chance." But every day in one's life, is an opportunity, a "chance." Some combination of circumstances, if but observed and utilized was the one thing needed to give the lesson for that day, and there are three hundred and sixty-five such days in every year, each twenty-four hours long.

When I was in the mission field in South Africa, the wife of one of our most active and useful ministers was herself active in mission work. Though a mother of a large family, she could be counted on to be present at various committee or club meetings, held in the interest of the general work. One of the things very much needed to make those meetings of sufficient interest and attraction to guarantee a good attendance of young people was to have singing, accompanied by the organ. But it happened so often there was no one present who could play, so Mrs. Gow determined to learn to play, that the difficulty might be removed. And she did. It required patience and severe application of the few hours that she could snatch each week from domestic duties, to practice on the organ.

Bishop Daniel A. Payne tells of how he acquired French outside of the school house. The fact is, the most he learned was outside of the school house. His biographer cites him as teaching a "High School" before he entered school at Gettysburg, the only regularly established school in which he ever studied. But men of recognized scholarship deemed it a privilege in after years to sit at his feet and learn wisdom, and the foremost educators of his day, men at the head of America's leading colleges and universities would refer to him as an "educator" on a plane with themselves, while Wilberforce University, the school that he established, and whose first president he was, has a name and a place among American institutions of learning.

Ex-President William McKinley and Frederick Douglass stood on the same platform together and received the degree of LL.D. at Wilberforce, and both seemed to appreciate highly the honor bestowed.

But the men whom I have named as illustrations of self-made men, such as Lincoln, Douglass, Payne, are all historic characters, and rated as being among the most illustrious of their times—and they were contemporary—but there are many others, practically unknown and unheralded who, on account of their acquirements and accomplishments; who on account of their influence upon society, have been as great beneficiaries to mankind as those whose fame took on national proportions. Their names are legion, for they are many. They are women and they are men, self-made but, splendidly made. Their school was the wide world, their books were men and things, and everything.

Hugh Miller, the noted Scotch geologist, in his "Schools and Schoolmasters"—autobiography—begins the narration with the story of a stout little boy in his sixth or seventh year, who was dispatched from an old-fashioned farm-house to drown a litter of puppies in an adjacent pond; who, after wasting some time in a paroxysm of indecision and sorrow, instead of committing the puppies to the water, tucked them up in his little kilt and set out by a blind pathway in a direction opposite to that of the farm-house. When he reached the home of his poor and widowed mother, she met him with raised hands, exclaiming: "What's this? What brings you here?" "The little doggies," was the prompt reply. "I couldna drown the little doggies." This is the index of character. The first examination in the big school. The boy made high marks, and began a career, with a bunch of puppies, which through an apparently trivial incident, "exercised a marked influence on the circumstances and destiny of at least two generations, higher in the seals than themselves." It is wonderful just how small things often entirely unnoticed, entering into one's life, contribute so much towards shaping one's destiny.

> "A little pebble in the river
> Has turned its course forever."

I met Mr. Douglass toward the end of his

illustrious career. Heard him speak. What
a speaker! I printed in the A. M. E. Review,
while editor of that periodical, several articles
by Mr. Douglass. Got to know him personally. He would reply to my letters as promptly and courteously, and give me a hearing as
readily as he would a man of national fame
like himself. With tender voice, he had a
word of encouragement for any young man,
or woman, who seemed to hold the right ideas
about life. and was striving to make something of himself. He seemed entirely incapable of manifesting a spirit of arrogance and
pride so often found in persons of less ability,
and with nothing of noble achievement to
boast of. He was the first of his race variety
in America to become a national and international character, and he completed a long and
useful career "without the smell of fire on his
garments."

I knew Bishop Payne much better. Indeed,
I knew him personally, and intimately, and
owe him more, and reverence him more than
any other man except my own dear father.

But there are others who, entering into, influenced my life for good to a very great
extent. Not being widely known outside of
their homes, they are not known to the

world. But their lives and deeds constitute some of the brightest and most interesting pages of unwritten history.

It is indeed a question whether men live longest and best in their own personal lives, or in the lives of those influenced by them. Perhaps it is in the lives of others, for, many may be started off on careers that are sure to accomplish more than any single life could.

The period of 1869-1877 was full of incidents, and decided my future course. These years were spent in the city of Wilmington, Del. Wilmington, in New Castle County, is the chief city in the Diamond State, Delaware. Delaware is a border state. The famous Mason and Dixon's Line divides between Delaware and Maryland, and Pennsylvania and Maryland.

Delaware was influenced by southern sentiment, and like Maryland, held slaves before the war. Adjacent to Pennsylvania, and being a small state, with but three counties, it has been suggested that it would be a good thing, politically, if Delaware State were a county in Pennsylvania. But the Claytons, Saulsburys, DuPonts and like celebrities would never agree to any such "demotion" for their proud little state, that even now, more than a half century after Emancipation, still retains the pillory and whipping post, though it is fair to say, that in this year of our Lord, 1919, a bill has been offered in the Legislature at Dover to have these relics of barbarism removed. I am advised that the bill failed to pass.

Since 1865, the year of the "surrender," and the beginning of great revolutions and changes in American politics, Delaware has been a "close" state, falling now into the hands of the Republicans, and now back into the Democratic column.

Wilmington had some colored men "of mark," who knew "Thomie Garrett, the Tatnels and other "Quakers" who were active in Underground Railroad service. Men, who, like Paul, were "free born." They were ready when Emancipation came, and the amendments to the Constitution followed, to organize the "freedman," instruct and coach him, and place him securely into the Republican fold.

My adventure into Delaware was just at a time that offered the opportunity to meet and mingle with those men, in the prime and strength of their lives, and when there were burning questions both as to church and state to be considered.

Daniel P. Hamilton, Daniel B. Anderson, David Augustus, Abraham Murray, William Grinnage and John Layton were among the leaders of thought among laymen in Wilmington. Frisby J. Cooper had entered the ministry and gone elsewhere. William Howard Day, from Oberlin College, the brilliant orator, handsome, well educated, a veritable Chesterfield in manners, came through occasionally while on speech-making tours. Later, he made Wilmington his home for a time, with his handsome wife, "Georgie," before they made Harrisburg their permanent home. He also became a minister and General Officer in the A. M. E. Zion Church. Ministers such as Dr. T. G. Stewart and John F. Thomas, of the A. M. E. Church; Edward Chippey, of the A. U. M. P. Church; Edward Williams, of the U. A. M. E. Church; Hooper Jolly, of the M. E. Church, were the leading churchmen. These were the four denominations among colored at that time. The men above-named, both laymen and ministers, were above reproach in character and above the average in ability, and enjoyed the confidence of the community— prerequisites for successful leadership. There were many others who deserve honorable

mention, but, as all cannot be named, these
are given as samples.

It was my good fortune to know these men
personally, to enjoy their confidence and respect; to be encouraged by them as a "likely"
young man; to be sought and brought forward to work with them in civic, religious and
political activities. It was my better fortune
to have been influenced by their lives. They
were men of thought and vision as well as
character.Solid men, who could be depended
upon to advocate a cause because it was good
and worthy, and not on account of what they
selfishly hoped to get out of it. They were big
men to me then, but much bigger now, as
from this distance I look back upon them.

Daniel P. Hamilton became my ideal in politics and religion. He was a "stand-pat" Republican, and a died-in-the-wool African
Methodist. He could wake up in the night
and give a reason for his faith both as to denomination and political party. He regarded
the abolitionists, and especially those of an active, Underground Railroad type, as being
worthy of the appellation "salt of the earth."
These were all Republicans, of course.

The Negro had his political birth in the
cradle of the Republican party and derived all

of his political privileges from that source, and
to Brother Hamilton, it was ingratitude to his
friends, and suicidal to himself, to leave the
party, or, to even be lukewarm toward it.
though we were yet deprived of many privileges and rights guaranteed and granted without question to other citizens under the Constitution. He used to tell a story about how a
woman changed her husband's politics. It was
like this: Upon a certain election day, he,
with certain others, were induced to vote the
Democratic ticket. The reward was a plenty
of whiskey and a barrel of flour. Early in the
day the flour came, but the prodigal husband
remained away from home all day where the
liquid refreshment flowed freely so long as the
polls were open. At last, much the worse for
wear, the prodigal returned, penitent, perhaps,
but too full for utterance. Well, wifey, assisted him in getting undressed and snugly
tucked in bed, and soon he was wrapped so
tightly in the arms of morpheus that he was
not even interested in the latest returns. This
was wife's opportunity to give him his first
lesson in political science. So, with strong
cords she lashed him fast to the bed, without
either his knowledge or consent. Then, taking a good-sized hickory club, she pounded him

so furiously and long that he died from his injuries. Of course she was arrested, and tried for murder. On the day of her trial, not having an advocate, she was permitted to speak for herself. She briefly rehearsed the story of her bondage. Told how children had been snatched from her embrace and sold to parts unknown. How she rejoiced when emancipated. And now that her husband was taking steps to have her again enslaved, she thought it was time to change his politics. When the judge heard her story, he instructed the jury to render a verdict of justifiable homicide. They did.

This is the atmosphere in which I took my first lessons in active politics. Here I cast my first vote. Twenty-one years of age was necessary to qualify as a voter but, if one had passed his twentieth when the election came off he could vote "on age." This was my case. I voted first on age and have never lost an opportunity since to cast my vote, and like my early political preceptors, I always vote "right." In theory, I am a Prohibitionist, but only in practice as it relates to drinking. I have always hoped that prohibition would come as a moral necessity, and not as a political measure. Politics are often a very uncertain quantity; at least politicians. The one party that had made it possible for the colored man to vote at all, was the Republican party, and it was both to its interest and ours, to keep the bond of union. I was never willing to hazard the success of the Republican ticket by voting any other, even the Prohibition ticket. Whenever there was a temperance plank in the Republican platform, such as local option, I was found a strong advocate and supporter. Indeed, my first public speech was a temperance address. To me it is a matter for great rejoicing that prohibition has triumphed to the extent, that more than two-thirds of the states have voted in favor of an amendment to the Constitution, that will banish from America its greatest foe, human slavery—the sum of all villainies—alone excepted. To me it is also a pleasure to know that this great triumph has come, not to the credit of any political party, but as a general uprising by the people to save the youth and to save the race. May the good work continue by being made a world-wide movement, for it does seem incredible, that in any part of the civilized world, so great an evil as the manufacture and sale of alcoholic liquors as a beverage, could have ever been legalized.

As in politics, so in religion, I came under
the influence of that masterful Daniel P. Hamilton. I was a Christian and a member of the
African Methodist Episcopal Church when I
met him, and had heard from the mouth of
"Father Jones" something about "Allen," and
what his Church stood for. But as a lad I had
not taken it so seriously that it had become
"second nature" with me. All of my Wilmington relatives belonged to other communions,
some to the M. E. and others to one or the
other of the "Union" churches. My home was
with those who belonged to the M. E. Church,
and I frequently accompanied them to "Ezion."

The young people of Wilmington were making much of the study of vocal music at that
time. In nearly every house one could hear
do, do, do; fa, fa, fa; sol, sol, sol. The churches
did not have organs then; all the music was
vocal, and the singers sang by note. Every
church had a good substantial choir, and the
singing was made a special feature of the
service. James Crozier, the leader of "Ezion"
choir, was the principal chorister among the
churches, and had regular weekly rehearsals,
where the members of the choir were required
to come and learn to read the notes. This was
very attractive to me, and I united with this

singing class, and much to my own delight began the study of vocal music. I thought about the Quimby class in the Cecilton school-house where I stood at the window and resolved that if ever I got a chance, I would study do, re, mi. Being encouraged by my own progress and becoming impatient with the backward ones who kept the class back, I resolved to take extra lessons from other masters, which I did; from Messrs. Peter S. Blake and James A. Anderson, at the same time attending the Crozier rehearsals weekly, and singing on "Ezion" choir.

My friends, Isaac Parker and Arso Purnell—members of the Crozier School—and I would frequently meet for private practice, and we considered it a great triumph when we could pick up the Jubilee, or, the New Lute of Zion, or, the Sacred Lute, and read any piece therein at sight. All the while I was attending Bethel A. M. E. Church as a member, and being a member of the Sunday school of which Daniel P. Hamilton was superintendent, becoming more acquainted with the man who in due time would fully and to my satisfaction explain the Allen movement, and enable me, like himself, to answer

the question, Why am I an African Methodist?

One warm—not to say hot—Sunday afternoon, I was on the choir at "Ezion," and the
pastor had given the service to an elderly
white minister who had evidently come
around, as they often did, looking for an opportunity to preach. After the preliminaries
were concluded and the brother got fairly
down to work at his sermon, which was evidently worked out for a "colored" congregation, he became illustrative, and used the following as pertinent to the occasion. "When I
was a boy I used to go to the kitchen where
the colored boys had a big fire. I would read
to them by the light of the candle. Who made
that fire? The colored boys. Who made the
candles? The white boys. And so, we come
to you for your fire, and you come to us for
our light." I looked around among the members of the choir to discover what effect this
injudicious—to say the least—comparison had
upon them. I discovered many of them had
been put soundly to sleep by his narcotized
homily, and others seemed not to have been
sufficiently interested to pay any attention at
all to what he was saying. Well, I decided
that I had shown sufficient gratitude to

Bro. Crozier for giving me an opportunity to study vocal music, and a chance to practice on the congregation of "Ezion" and that this insult to my manhood would be a sufficient explanation should I ever be asked why I discontinued my membership in the choir. So right in the midst of the discourse at the conclusion of that personal application, I took my hat and unceremoniously left the church. I then became an active member of Bethel Choir, and when during the next year, our leader, Josiah Loans, died, I was unanimously elected by the members of the choir to succeed him. I am not quite sure that the Mayor-elect of the city of Wilmington felt more highly honored in his elevation than I did in mine. I was well aware of my limitations as master chorister, but of two things I felt sure; my connection with the choir for more than a year gave me a chance to know that no one there was better prepared for the place than myself, and, that if severe application would do the deed, I would be sure to keep ahead of the rest of them.

The minister who impressed me most at this really formative period of my life was Dr. Theophilus Gould Steward. I cannot say that I listened very critically to sermons previous

to the time that he became my pastor. To me,
preaching was in a way, professional oratory,
of a more or less emotional style, and the
preacher who could entertain the people agree-
ably, and make them happy most of the time,
was to me, the right man in the right place.
If he were not thus gifted as a speaker, the
consensus of opinion was, it would be better
for the spiritual growth of the Church if his
pastorate covered but one or two years. But
the advent of Dr. Steward marked the turning
point of my idea of preaching. Strange to say,
his style made him exactly the opposite of
what had been my ideal, if indeed, I had given
sufficient thought to the subject to have what
might be dignified as an ideal. If any one became very demonstrative under the preaching
of Dr. Steward, it was more on account of
what he said than his manner of saying it. He
had none of the "rousnum" that a "Methodist
Preacher" was supposed to have, and to bring
in at least, toward the close of his sermon if
not before. It was the custom of many to pay
but little attention to the beginning of the
sermon. Indeed, they would often fix themselves for a quiet nap, while the preacher was
making preliminary remarks, and warming
up, but would be wide-awake in time to see

the finish, and join in the hallelujahs that generally closed this part of the service.

The Steward style was not popular from the first with the masses. Many adverse criticisms could be heard upon the style of the new preacher. Some characterized him as a Presbyterian, and others as a lecturer. Dr. Steward knew perfectly well what was going on, but he also knew what the people needed, and paid no attention to the criticisms of those who were no more capable of sitting in judgment upon a theological discourse, or denominational tenets, than they were upon geology, or political economy. Our minister began to make friends and converts to his way of thinking, and his manner of expressing his thoughts. As for me, I found myself so absorbed in what I heard from the pulpit Sunday after Sunday, and from the lesson reviews and addresses in the Sunday school by our pastor, and in personal conversation in social as well as official life, that there was no place so attractive to me as Bethel Church, and no services so helpful as the Sunday morning services, where sermons, fresh, well prepared, and delivered more and more forcefully as the response from the pew was more cordial, became the very bread of life to the soul and a means of enlightenment to the mind.

The friendship between Bro. D. P. Hamilton and myself became closer and stronger, and it was his delight to push me forward in the affairs of the church, especially in the Sunday school, where for many years he had been the superintendent. My fondness of Bible study, and my knowledge of, and love for vocal music, made the Sunday school to me a very desirable place. The International Lessons were just being introduced into Sunday schools, and we laid aside the old system of study and adopted the Berean series of the International Course. My practice was to study each lesson in connection with the Home Readings; parallel passages and Scriptural references; the English Teacher's Notes; topic, title, golden text and Teacher's Quarterly, Peloubet's Select Notes, and whatever I could get, throwing light upon the lessons, and upon the Scriptures generally. This became a habit with me, and year in and year out I kept it up, thus acquiring a general familiarity with the Bible, The Old Book; "lamp unto my feet, and a light unto my path." Psalms 119.

My cousin, Christopher Jones, and I, used to teach each other by each reading passages from the Bible, Old and New Testaments, and asking the other to name the book—author—from which the passage was read. The Bible has been my chief text book for the preparation of life's work. It is art, science and literature—geology, astronomy, biology, geography, ethnology, biography, history, sociology, hygiene, and above all, theology. God, man's relation to his Maker, his whence and his whither. What a book! All other books are but parts of this great book of nature, and revelation.

As my progress in learning proceeded largely by dint of hard study and application, my brick yard experience became an important period in my life. Machinery for making bricks had not then come fully into vogue. Nearly all bricks for building purposes were hand made. The men even dug the clay with spades instead of the steam shovels now used. These fellows of the clay bank had a wonderful appetite and a marvelous digestion. Some of them boasted that they could digest an oyster shell.

From a child I was of slender build; not muscular. But a few years on the brickyard of James Beggs laid for me a physical foundation upon which I am now supporting a building weighing two hundred and forty-seven pounds, more than sixty pounds above my father's best weight, and still more in advance of any other member of the family. The old brick moulders said, that in order to become a master workman one must come into the yard when a boy, and learn to "off bear" and all that was preliminary to moulding. There was a sort of aristocracy among the brick mould-ers, as there was among the grain measurers of long ago. Men who did not go into the yards when a boy and "come up," never got beyond "wheelers." Well, some one must prove to be an exception, and as I always had an independent way about doing things, I de-cided to become an innovation in the art of "rolling a walk," and taking a near cut, be-come a brick moulder. And so I did. It was only a round table talk for a little while, for when I could turn out two thousand, three hundred and thirty-two—"a day's task in four hours," the speediest record attained, the old veterans admitted me into their society by simply admitting that I had done the "impos-sible." One who could finish his task in from four to six hours, had a good deal of leisure each day. My custom was to begin work at four o'clock in the morning, and this gave me much time for study. Earning wages above the average wage earner, with a brick-yard appetite, and the ability and inclination to sleep the sleep of the just, and the invigorating value of early morning air and exercise, I was prepared to make the most of my hours of leisure, and I have always been able to look back with satisfaction upon the days when the music of the steel mould was the early morning song on the brick-yard.

Having saved some money, after a few years on the brick-yard, I decided to go into business with a company of young men who were like minded. So, a place on Shipley Street, above Eighth, was selected, and there under the rather pretentious firm name of "Collins, Coppin & Co.," we opened a retail flour business. The outfit consisted of a store-room, with the regulation counter and shelves, and a coal stove. A few barrels of flour were purchased; a number of small cotton bags for handling small quantities of five and ten pounds to be delivered to customers, emptied, and the bags retained. Upon the shelves were placed a quantity of articles for the accommodation of customers who might become regular purchasers of flour; articles such as soap, starch, some canned goods, tea, coffee and sugar.

It soon became apparent that if we would compete with other retail flour merchants we must, like them, deliver the goods to the homes of our customers. For this necessity, a horse and wagon were purchased. Then, too, an order occasionally would come in for a barrel of flour which could only be delivered by the use of a horse and wagon.

Now with a complete outfit the business opened auspiciously. Cash customers came around in numbers sufficient to make the business attractive and the company optimistic. The customers increased, the receipts increased. Quite a number of customers opened weekly accounts. As is generally the case, the credit orders became larger than the cash orders by the same customer. For a time the weekly payments were promptly made, and the number of such customers, as well as the size of the orders increased. This, of course, worked no hardships, for the firm could easily get monthly credit and besides, it was business, as the Saturday receipts showed, and business was the thing we opened for. But alas! we had our lesson to learn. A lesson that can only be learned by experience. After the credit accounts mounted up into hundreds of dollars, one after another of the largest buyers failed to come around on pay day. Good excuses and good promises followed, but these were not made good. The result was inevitable. The business finally closed down with large outstanding bills that even the professional and astute collecting agencies could not collect. The company wound up its affairs, wiser, poorer, and with fewer friends, but with an experience that was sure to be turned to good account.

My next venture was at school teaching. A teacher was needed at Smyrna, Del. I applied to the Actuary, Mr. Henry Conrad, later, the Hon. Henry Conrad, and obtained the place. Smyrna was and still is a flourishing little town. The "two races" got on peaceable together and both prospered. "Uncle" Lewis Hamilton was to Smyrna, in a general way, and to our Church in particular, what his illustrious brother was to Wilmington, and to its church life: in both cases, meaning first of all, the African Methodist Episcopal Church. At Smyrna, I was day school teacher: Sunday School General Director, and Assistant; teacher of vocal music, and, in fact, a sort of plenipotentiary in all matters social, moral and intellectual. I was hailed as a sort of envoy extraordinary; consulted upon all matters, and pushed forward in all the secular and religious activities. I may have been of some benefit to the people of Smyrna, but the opportunity afforded me for intellectual and administrative development, was of incalculable benefit to me. It afforded the needed opportunity for research and study, both as it related to leisure and favorable vocation. And being called upon to enter into all the local activities of whatever nature, taking the leading part, the result was, theory and practice most admirably combined. This new leadership, with its responsibilities, gave me a chance to better understand the kind of equipment needed, and how to obtain it. Many a learned man cannot teach school; cannot organize, cannot govern, cannot initiate. Blessed is he who has the talent and gift for those things, and the learning besides. The kind of education most needed and how to impart it, is one of the very much alive questions of the day. It is now reduced to a science, but some of our most successful educators had to work it out along lines of common sense, thanks to that inventive genius called necessity.

The first and only time I ever saw Henry

Ward Beecher was in a lecture at the Academy of Music, Philadelphia, on "The New Profession." He made it quite clear to my mind that there were persons teaching school who were not following their calling. He suggested that school teachers should be better paid, and then required to give efficient and conscientious service, thus making it an honorable and profitable "profession," instead of a means to an end. Teaching school offers an opportunity for character study. Children in school are passing the most impressionable and the most indefinite period of their lives. "A little pebble in the river has often turned its course forever." It causes a very comfortable feeling to have a man or woman in after life meet you, and say: "I attribute my success in life to the fact that I came under your influence at an early period of my life."

William Whartenbury and the Hemsley girls, and David Clayton, are about all of my old Smyrna pupils, as I remember it now, who are still living at Smyrna. "Bill Tom Hill" moved to Wilmington, Del., and reared his family. John Price, my brightest pupil, went away to teach. I have lost sight of him. The children and grandchildren of "Uncle" Lewis Hamilton who still live are scattered. John

Purnell teaches school in New Jersey. His sister Anna—sweet girl—died before reaching her majority. Whartenbury comes to Philadelphia to see his children and grandchildren. "Uncle" Wesley Brown's Richard started off on a brilliant business career but was overtaken by death. My old friend, Joseph Whaley, has passed away. All the Potts family have disappeared. Smyrna has grown much larger since those days. It was my privilege to visit there a little while ago, note familiar scenes and look into the few familiar faces that remain "to remind us of the past." But it was the old Smyrna that impressed me, through its stalwart, historic characters, who have since passed away.

It was here that I first met the Hon. John S. Durham. Not then the able diplomat and counselor-at-law, but a beardless youth, teaching his first school in an adjacent school district in the same county as Smyrna. He and I became friends and companions. A braver lad never faced American prejudice. On one Sunday he came into Smyrna, and went to the M. E. Church (white) and took a seat in the gallery. He noticed that his presence caused some commotion. The next day a "gentleman" from Smyrna drove down to his school, and advised him, for his personal safety, to not repeat the visit. But, it took my additional advice, forcefully given , to dissuade him.

After my friend Durham had grown too large for the Kent County school and large enough for the editorial staff of the Philadelphia Bulletin, and I had become pastor of "Mother Bethel Church," we met at a bazaar at the Eleventh Street Masonic Hall, in Philadelphia, and he challenged me for a bet that I would not offer to accompany Miss Fanny M. Jackson home from the Bazaar. The sequel of this rash challenge, and the still more rash venture on my part will constitute some of the pages in another chapter.

Reference to my stay in Wilmington, Del., would be incomplete without acknowledging my debt of gratitude due to my own dear relatives with whom I lived.

My home was with John Backus, the husband of my Aunt Clara, one of the "shoestring-breed" girls of Amelia Lily, my maternal grandmother. They reared but one child, Amanda, who was the wife of Benjamin Mislis, and lived home with her parents. They had buried a number of children, and seemed afraid to permit Amanda to go from them.

She was, indeed, the sunshine of the home, and everybody deferred to her. She was to me a model woman, and housekeeper and Christian.

Uncle John and Aunt Clara were like bride and groom. In the seven years I spent in their home, I never heard a harsh word passed between either couple. Uncle John was especially affectionate. I got an idea that I wanted to be such a husband. Here I spent the first years of my early manhood; here in this model, Christian home. My first home away from the Cecilton fireside. Here the moral atmosphere was pure, and love abounded, and the influence could only be salutary. These dear ones have passed away, but they still live in the lives of others.

CHAPTER VI.

My Call to the Ministry

Are poets born? Are lawyers and doctors and statesmen called? One way to judge a man's calling is by what he can do well. No one would doubt that music was the calling of "Blind Tom." As much may be said of many others who have become experts, or famous in certain lines of endeavor. But, I mean something quite different when I speak of a call to the ministry. Both in the Old Testament and the New, there is no fact more plainly stated than the fact that the Prophets, Judges, Apostles and Disciples were specifically called to their work; and there is nothing stated or inferred in the Bible, nor suggested by reason, to cause one to conclude that the Almighty has ever changed His method of bringing into service those who are to proclaim and to interpret His word. "And no man taketh this honor unto himself, but he that is called of God, as was Aaron." This statement in Hebrews is an evidence that the inspired writer of that book that has so much to say about the priesthood, held the same view concerning a Divine call to the ministry that I am representing.

For a long time the thought lingered with me that my life work was to be the ministry, but for reasons, many, I would banish the thought. The most valid reason that I can give was a fear that I was mistaken in the impression that seemed to linger with me. Having a natural reverence for divine things, with rather a religious bent, and a fondness for Bible study, and besides, some one to remark now and again that I was "cut out for the ministry," I felt that it might be an easy thing to drift into this sacred work, regarding it as any other profession that one might take up. This very thought was revolting to me. As an officer in the church, and member of the Quarterly Conference, where candidates for the ministry were examined, I was rather severe on those who came before us, claming to have been "called to the work."

I remember on one occasion, an applicant for license expressed himself as being quite sure that he "heard a voice," very distinctly calling him. My friend, Daniel P. Hamilton

and I, both members of the Quarterly Conference in question, were quite amused by this
declaration, and after subjecting our candidate to a veritable "third degree" examination,
he disappeared and never returned to us, to
renew his request for license, or to stand an
examination. But he did unite with another
church of the same denomination, from which
he obtained license, and became a fairly accept-
able, and fairly successful traveling preacher,
especially when he "traveled" from place
to place and avoided long pastorates at any
one place. He was very much limited in educational ability, and did not seem to fully appreciate the need of "preparation" that even
a "called" man must make. Doubtless he was
conscientious, even if mistaken upon some
points. But after rather enjoying the distinction of being a "terror" to those who applied for license to preach I had to face an
impression, that became as real as the fact
that it was my duty to live an honorable life.
It became so real, that I was afraid not to
yield. It was no longer a question to me as
to whether or not I was called, but, whether
or not I would be "disobedient to the heaven-
ly calling." I faltered once, even after I was
thoroughly convinced, and paid the price of

a depression of spirit, and sense of condemnation that I hope never to witness again.

In my anguish, I promised, that if the shadow was lifted, and I permitted again, even for a moment to enjoy peace of heart, I would openly declare my purpose to go into the work. The peace returned: a conscious peace! Perhaps further details would not be interesting to the reader. Suffice it to say, that the cause of the depression of spirit, and also what gave relief, were both perfectly clear to me, and there has not been a moment in the forty-three years since, that I have doubted either. It has been this conscientious conviction of being in the line of duty, that has nerved me to do my best. I have ever since felt like one to whom had been committed a sacred trust to which I was bound by every consideration of honor to be true and faithful. But even more; I have always felt that it was a trust that could not be relinquished. A case of "woe is me if I preach not the gospel." Concerning any other calling, or profession, one may feel at liberty to lay it aside at pleasure, and take up something more pleasant, more lucrative, more desirable. Not so with the really called minister. "No man, having put his hand to the plough, and looking back, is fit for the Kingdom of God." Much is being said of late about the fewness of young men, especially school men who enter the ministry, and the cause generally suggested, is, that business and professional pursuits are more lucrative. I cannot think of a better reason for staying out of the ministry than a desire to obtain a lucrative position. This was not promised to nor enjoyed by the Prophets, the apostles, nor our Divine Master. To the contrary, the rule was, to give up much for a calling that promised nothing in particular of earthly gain. Even now, in this age, where the material is put forward and valued so often, not to say generally, to the neglect of the spiritual, there are men who deliberately, and from choice, turn away from well paying positions, to the uncertain temporal reward of a traveling preacher. But for the consciousness of a divine calling such a step would be unwise in the extreme, and would probably never be taken.

There are false Prophets, and teachers. Of this our Lord has warned us. Men have entered the ministry for a life of ease. For a life that would not be characterized by physical toil. Some, with a desire for the fleece, instead of the flock, have become self consti-

tuted shepherds. All such have brought a reproach upon the ministry, and so lowered the
standard thereof, that many have stood aloof,
who otherwise would have followed a conscious leading in that direction. Many who
have not learned the lesson of self denial, have
come professionally, with unchanged hearts,
into the ministry; because, in spite of misrepresentation, and false representatives, the
ministry has won for itself a social distinction,
that places it at once in the rank of respect-
ability. The supposition is, that ministers are
men of pure lives, and motives, and they are
therefore freely admitted into good society and
given the confidence of husbands, and wives,
and children, without suspicion. It is taken
for granted that they are honorable and honest in business transactions, and are not held
strictly to the C. O. D. business rules generally
in vogue. It is easy then, for a false, design-
ing, and morally weak individual to enter this
open door of confidence and bring reproach
upon the cause. These are the things, more
than the consideration of "wages" that deter
true and honest men from entering the ministry. Those "learned" ones, who object simply on account of uncertain material compen-

sation, do well to follow the secular callings for which alone they are prepared.

I entered the ministry in the spring of '77, from the church that I had learned to love so much. The church in whose Sunday school I had studied the scriptures consecutively and constantly year by year. In whose official Board I had become familiar with church polity and discipline. The church that because it believed in me, had brought me forward as its representative on all important occasions, and had exercised patience, and charity in the face of my many blunders and short comings. My first adopted chruch home: Bethel, in Wilmington, Del.

Rev. John F. Thomas was the pastor. Bishop Daniel A. Payne was the Presiding Bishop of the Philadelphia Annual Conference of which the churches in Deleware were a part.

My first charge was "The Philadelphia City Mission." This circuit of Missions consisted of three points, namely, Morris Brown Mission, at Vineyard and Poplar Sts., Philadelphia; St. James Mission, in the fourth story of a big hall, with bar room on the first floor; dancing hall on the second; lodge room on the third and my Mission on the fourth. The third point was at Seventy-second St., and Greenway Ave

in that portion of the city known as King-
sessing, or Pascalville. The Mission house
was a small wooden building, about fifteen
by twenty feet, with straight weather boarding, and being not stripped, the boards inclined to separate, thus affording light and venti-
lation, which worked well in summer, but was
neither necessary nor desirable for winter.

My membership at Morris Brown was
eighteen communicants with a promising Sunday school of twenty or thirty, consisting
principally of small children, with a number
of young misses, and a few young men. The
Mission being in the northwestern portion of
the city, in the direction of and not far from
the home of Dr. B. T. Tanner, Editor of the
Christian Recorder, his entire family attended
Sunday school there; the children were converted there and inducted into the Church
proper. Henry O.: celebrated artist. Hally:
wife, mother, physician, Mary: lawyer's wife;
mother; having now the care of her father
in his declining years.

Carlton: Minister, author, distinguished as
preacher and financier.

Isabella: Minister's wife and Missionary
worker.

Sarah: named for her mother; Professor's wife; mother.

Bertha: Physician's wife; mother.

All went thru the Philadelphia High Schools before taking their higher courses for professional work.

It is conceded by all who know the Tanner family, that it consists of an unusual set of children altogether, with one towering as an international character. They entered the Church in childhood, from a Christian home, characterized by the simple life, where a pack of cards would have been unceremoniously thrown into the fire; a parlor dance regarded as sacralige; whiskey, wine and beer, as a desecration. No tobacco; no vulgarity; no profanity. Family prayers and early to bed, and early to school. True all of this might be observed withqut producine an ideal family, but it is about what Scripture prescribes, and reason suggests.

Morris Brown Mission looks back with much delight upon the fact that so distinguished a family had its first Sunday school and Church training there. So does Morris Brown Mission's pastor. The Morris Brown people in general thought much of themselves as families and churchmen. They gave

certain caste to the Church that still charac-
terizes it. They did not practice undue emotionalism in worship. They were Bible readers: Sunday-school goers: class and prayer-
meeting advocates, in precept and example.
Willing workers and liberal givers to the support of the Church, local and connectional.
They started right, and kept right. The Tan-
ners, and Moors, and Browns, and Telegrones,
and Mears', and Orrs and Thomas', and Mid-
dletons, and Nichols', and Frys, and Henrys'
and Parkers and Dades and Butlers. And
many others who came later, and are there
still.

What about St. James, the second named
in the Philadelphia Mission Circuit? Well,
it was up too high. By the advice of Bishop
Payne, I soon dissolved it, took as many members to Morris Brown as would go, and advised that the contingent that came from
Union Church, Fifth and Fairmount Avenue,
return.

The Third in the triumvirate, at Seventy-
second and Greenway Ave., like Morris Brown
still remains; alive and healthy. Both self-
supporting stations. Were made so too soon
however, for the burdens that they have carried for years, have militated against their

growth. Mr. Thomas Hooper and his wife became the principal supporters of the King-
sessing Church from the very beginning, and
without them I think St. John never would
have stemmed the current. Theirs was the
home of the ministers from year to year.
The boarding house for visitors on quarterly
meeting and all special occasions. He acting
sexton, even to the extent of often furnishing
fuel: his wife "Elenora" filling his place at
his absence. They lived directly in the rear
of the Church on Hooper street: named for
Mr. Hooper. The little Church first stood on
the rear of the lot, and looked the Hooper
residence in the face. Even now that the
Church fronts on Greenway Avenue, there is
a back entrance to Hooper street: or, to be
more exact, to the Hooper residence.

After my first year on the Philadelphia City
Mission work, Morris Brown, plucky Morris
Brown, asked to be set apart to itself, and her
pastor returned, which request was granted
by the Conference, and Morris Brown, to the
delight of her founders, became a Mission
Station.

The request of the Mission, and act of the
Conference in granting it was fully justified
by the growth of the charge during the follow-

ing year. The Sunday school increased four-
fold. The membership increased to sixty-five,
and a building fund of five hundred dollars
was placed in the Spring Garden bank, looking forward to purchasing a Church site. We
worshipped in the second story of a little hall,
the ground floor of which was used as a Marble yard. Our little room was quite fixed up
with organ, piano, Sunday school library, carpet for the floor, and curtains for the windows.
We were the first Church in the Philadelphia
Conference to not only hand to the Conference a dollar from each member for the General Fund, but even more dollars than we had
members. I believe the Church still leads in
dollar money percentage.

The Mission Station preacher went to Conference with a brand new suit of clothes, and
—laughable to confess—cut in the regular
Ministerial style, and he a Licentiate. Could
not baptise, lawfully, a sick baby, though he
did so once in spite of the law, reported it to
his Presiding Elder and was not censured.

Having served two years, according to Disciplinary regulations, and having also made the
course of studies prescribed for the Deaconite
I was ordained Deacon at my second Conference.

The Philadelphia Conference that year was held at Reading, Penna., a German town. When world war involved the United States and every body was ordered to curse the Kaiser, and speak evil of all Germans, it was not quite safe to speak the German language, much less was it safe to speak in complimentary terms of the German people. But, the war is over now; let us hope forever, and it may not be out of place to say, that Reading, and other German settlements, welcomed and entertained our Conferences royally. All hotels were open to us, the same as to others. All the Churches were thrown open, and our ministers invited to preach. On this particular occasion, I accompanied Dr. T. G. Steward to a "white" Church. His text was: "Thou shall call his name Jesus, for he shall save his people from their sins." Dr. Steward preached a characteristic sermon which was most favorably commented upon afterwards. Not only were hotels open to us as to others, but homes, as is the custom among Christian people when a religious gathering is coming to town. I only recall one other place where homes were placed at the disposal of Conference members, and that is Millville, New Jersey.

The pastor of Mother Bethel Church was ill

during the session of Conference; so much so, that he couldn't be sent to a new charge, though he was physically unable to do the work of Bethel. So, the Bishop decided to let him remain and send a young, unmarried man there to assist him, "until" said he, "we see what the Lord will do with Whitfield." A council was held between the Bishop and his Elders and it was decided that "Young Coppin" was the man to send temporarily to Bethel. Of this decision I was promptly informed by the Bishop, and kindly, but firmly directed to go in the spirit of meekness, preach, visit the sick and bury the dead as an assistant, and by no means imagine myself the pastor. Only by the most inexcusable presumption could I entertain a thought of ascending to the pastorate of the Mother Church, even accidentally. I was only a Deacon, just ordained at that Conference, and with but two years experience, and that too with Mission points. But as human nature is capable of doing the unexpected and unreasonable at any time, the Bishop's advice and caution was not out of place.

Conference closed and sure enough, I was sent to Bethel as an assistant to the Rev. George C. Whitfield who was returned, leaning on his staff in the last stages of consumption. In less time than two weeks, Rev. Whitfield passed away, and by a vote of the official Board the Bishop was requested to let me remain until he held his New England Conference sixty days hence, at which time he promised to send a pastor to Bethel.

How would I spend those two months? Simply preaching, visiting the sick and burying the dead is by no means the sum of a Methodist preacher's duty. Our Churches are generally in debt, or, in need of repairs, or, without parsonage; something, however, that requires money, and the minister in our Churches is expected to plan and execute the financial rallies.

It happened that Bethel had a chronic debt. Not a large one to be sure, but one that on account of long standing, and supposed mismanagement, the people had repudiated. They claimed that money had been raised again and again for the debt, and put to other purposes, and for that reason they would not respond to collections for trustee purposes. The amount was twenty-seven hundred dollars, and the claim was held by a Fraternal Society. Besides this note, there were open accounts amounting to a few hundred dollars, making in all an indebtedness of over three thousand dollars.

I was no sooner installed for my two months pastorate, than the news was broken to me about this chronic indebtedness. Some were accusing and some excusing the trustees for its existence. Some also were accusing the ex-pastor for taking no interest in it, while others were saying that he did right to stand aloof, and not take sides with either of the contending parties. I saw no chance for doing much good spiritually or materially during my brief pastorate with a divided Church, so I concluded that the most that I could hope to accomplish in so brief a period as two months, would be to bring about a measure at least of harmony between the discordant elements.

The plan I fell upon was to call a Church meeting, have a season of song and prayer, then frankly talk matters over, avoiding so far as possible controversy. The meeting was called, was well attended. A more or less good feeling prevailed. I succeeded in convincing them that nothing could ever be gained by delaying payment of the indebtedness. It would never be repudiated, and the longer it stood, the larger it would grow. That it would be to the interest of all to settle the claims, and remove the unpleasant feeling that they had caused.

We agreed upon a plan, organized our forces and went to work. It was soon apparent, that the plan would succeed if not interrupted. And more; the way the people, young and old, were coming together and co-operating, it seemed evident that peace and harmony would soon prevail again at this old citadel of African Methodism: this fortress of religious enthusiasm: this source of manhood Christianity.

The older members, Shadd, Tate, Lawrence, Banton, Seymour, Frisby, Robinson and others who had fought many battles, and passed through many stormy scenes since 1816, were quick to discover if the present tendency continued it would lead to high tide of success, spiritually and materially, and they began to plan to have the two months' limit removed, and the Coppin pastorate made permanent. But how could this be done? The faithful membership at Morris Brown Mission had from the Bishop a promise that I was only borrowed for a time, and would soon be returned to them. Besides, I was only a Deacon. How could the Mother Church accept less than a full fledged minister as a regular pastor? But Bethel Pioneers were not to be defeated in their purpose.

So far as a Deacon filling the pulpit was concerned, they regarded that as only sentimental, and therefore not an insuperable difficulty. As to the Bishop's promise, that was quite another thing. But even facing this difficulty, they determined to not be thwarted in their purpose without exhausting their diplomatic skill.

When Bishop Payne was approached upon the subject, the messengers received a prompt and positive no; with two reasons; both reasons characteristic of Bishop Payne. "In the first place," said he. "You certainly do not mean to ask your Bishop to lie: I have promised his people at Morris Brown that he would return to them. Besides this, I do not want to spoil that young man, who might otherwise, be useful to the Church." This seemed decisive. But not with "Father" Tate. He promptly reminded the Bishop that if the people at the Morris Brown Mission would consent to the promotion, emphasizing "promotion," that he, the Bishop, would be free from his promise: and if those people loved· their pastor so well this would be a good way

to show it. As to the other objection, they
had no fear that he would be spoiled. "I have
watched the young man," said "Father" Tate,
"and from my knowledge and experience in
such matters, I am willing to assume all responsibility in this case.

When the Committee discovered that the
Bishop was considering the proposition, they
suggested the appointment of a committee to
wait on the Morris Brown people, to solicit
their consent. To this the Bishop agreed and
appointed Author Tate, W. C. Banton and Rev.
H. A. Knight then pastor of Union A. M. E.
Church, Philadelphia. "Uncle" George W. P.
Custic an enthusiastic advocate of the proposition made himself a self-constituted member
of the committee, and actually became its
spokesman. The Morris Brown people could
not withstand the logic and persuasive arguments of the committee, and so yielded and
my second ministerial appointment became
Mother Bethel. Bishop Payne never would
take to himself the credit of the appointment,
but always said, the Lord made it.

As for me: well, no one was more disappointed. I had already set my heart upon
securing a site for a Church, and leading the
people out of "Monumental Hall' and be-

sides, Morris Brown was to me a very large and important pastorate, and I was delighted to return to it. When I planned the rally at Bethel, I had not the slightest dream of doing more than bringing the people together, and putting the movement on foot preparatory to the coming of the new pastor.

It may not be generally known that the ground upon which Bethel Church stands, is the first piece of ground owned in America by an independent organization of our race variety. It is true that when the colored contingent of St. George Church withdrew, and a committee was appointed to purchase, or, select a church site, the one selected by Absolum Jones was accepted by the congregation, and not the one selected by Richard Allen. But, a majority of those who withdrew from St. George, thus forming the new congregation, voted to be Episcopalians, and St. Thomas was erected upon the lot chosen. St. Thomas Church is a part of the Protestant Episcopal Denomination, and not an independent congregation.

When the majority following Richard Allen organized, they accepted the lot that was purchased by him and reported at the original meeting. It is upon this lot that Bethel

Church is built; the first Church of the first organization in America with absolute independent ownership, and controlled by colored Americans.

When in September, 1908, sixteen religious denominations assembled to take part in the two hundred and twenty-fifth anniversary of the founding of Philadelphia, the writer was selected to represent all of the colored Denominations, upon the theme: "Penn and Religious Liberty." The addresses were necessarily brief, limited to the same number of minutes for delivery, and all read twice, the second time being to an overflow meeting where a second large building filled to overflow received each speaker as in his turn he came from the first building.

Sitting in a row in the large Friend's Meeting House, were the representatives of the following denominations, in the following order:

Universalists, Mennonites, Friends—Hixte—Colored Churches, Presbyterian, Baptist, Episcopalian, Roman Catholic, Hebrew, Lutheran, Congregational, Friends—Orthodox, Reformed, Methodist, Unitarian, Disciples.

My address, was, by the very nature of things, more an address on behalf of a people than a denomination, though it would be quite out of place to speak of the early struggles of a race for religious liberty, without referring to the pioneer of the movement.

The address follows:

Mr. Chairman:—Viewed from any standpoint, William Penn must be considered one of the foremost men of his age, and a good example for men of every age.

Refusing to take the condition of his illustrious father, Admiral Penn, and follow the fortunes of war, he chose for himself an ideal that constantly appealed to the highest and best instinct of his nature, and with admirable courage, made that ideal the guiding star of his eventful life.

Providently, it would seem, it became his lot to tread a new path and do initiative work in a new field, instead of undertaking the very uncertain task of changing old conditions and customs in an old and long established government.

It was fortunate for the new State which he was destined to found that his religious bent was settled and fixed before he entered upon the perplexing work of its organization and development.

The time was ripe for breaking away from

old forms of government where privileged classes took the place of true democracy, and the leader of such an important movement must needs be one whose sense of religious obligation would enable him to withstand the almost irresistible tide of popular sentiment.

It sometimes happens, that a people who are themselves fleeing from political and religious oppression, will become forgetful of the golden rule when they themselves become dispensers of the law.

In the day when Penn launched his ship of state, the evil of human slavery had not only received the sanction of the potentates of the Old World, but had dragged its debauching form into the New.

A writer of those times speaks thus: "Queen Elizabeth had the honor of extending the commerce of England to the slave-pens of the gold coast, and long before her time, in continental countries, anything made in the image of God, in a black skin, was considered property." Continuing, he says: "Slaves were held by all the American colonies, and if a man did not own slaves it was because he was too poor to buy them."

Here, then, was the soil into which William Penn must sow the seed of his ideal commonwealth and organize a government that must stand for religious liberty, civic righteousness, and the new doctrine proclaimed by the friends that "God has made men peers, and that seting up marks of separation was but dividing men without a cause, and trifling with the noblest work of God."

That the new venture would be sure to meet with numerous obstacles, must have been evident. How well it succeeded, the story of 225 years of effort must tell.

In 1688, at the Friends' meeting-house in Germantown, a protest was made against slavery, and although its success at first was not all that was hoped for, it was the "leaven in a measure of meal" that continued to work until the blight of slavery was finally banished forever from our fair land.

Thus it was that the city founded by Penn became the cradle of abolitionism, and the Society with which he had identified himself amid much persecution became a most potent force against the evil that has been fitly styled "the sum of all villianies."

But in answering the question: "William Penn's contribution to religious liberty," it will be well to ascertain who in his day was considered eligible to profess religion.

The status of a Negro, as a moral being, was undecided. Indeed, it was generally agreed that he was but a higher order of the beast creation, and that his brain was minus the gray matter that would entitle him to a place among men in the realm of thought.

Be it said, to the everlasting credit of the Society of Friends, that after a mighty wrestling, like Jacob, with their conscience, they were the first to discover that the Negro was nothing more nor less than a human being with an immoral soul.

Daniel Pastorious and others advised that Friends be careful not to encourage the bringing in of any more Negroes, and that such as had them should be careful to bring them to meetings and to restrain them from loose living.

In the year 1700, William Penn introduced a bill in the Council to regulate the morals and marriages of the Negroes, with this significant injunction: "Friends should be very careful in discharging a good conscience toword the Negroes and Indians in all respects." Following this injunction, a meeting was appointed for them once a month, which marked an epoch in the religious life of the African in America.

This forward movement in the interest of God's sable children proved to be seed sown in good ground, and bore its first fruit in the city where it was set in motion.

The soul, once unfettered, began that growth and development that lifts a human being into his proper sphere.

The idea of religious liberty, that was all pervading, found a response in these newly awakened souls and a change began to take place.

In 1787, a blacksmith shop became their meeting-house, and in the true spirit of William Penn they made a historic struggle for religious independence.

Out of the smoke and ashes of that humble beginning grew an organization that now numbers nearly a million souls, and upon the very spot where stood the blacksmith shop stands a spacious building, modern in all its appointments: a building, eloquently telling its own story of what a people may do when given an opportunity.

History bears testimony to the fact, that in every great movement in the unfolding of the divine plan for the betterment of society, God always finds a man whom He can rely upon as a leader.

Richard Allen, himself once a slave, became an apostle of the doctrine of religious liberty among his people, and it was through him that they were led on from a handful to a great religious denomination.

When Philadelphia is compared with other cities of the country for churches, and schools, and libraries, and hospitals, and organized charities, and institutions for the protection of dumb animals, and kindred societies, I think it will not suffer in comparison.

That the moral and religious forces set in action by the Founders of the city—and especially by its great Founder—still have their influence upon the city's life, there can be no reasonable doubt.

The statue of William Penn upon the city's highest monument, visible to all, and overlooking all, is a constant declaration, that the principles for which he stood are the principles by which we hope still to be guided.

The inhabitants of the City find no good reason to change the name given by its illustrious Founder.

The spirit of fair play and equal justice to all is still the dominant spirit.

Those who from afar visit the city of Brotherly Love during these series of celebrations, will do well to imbibe her spirit, and carry to the uttermost parts of America the doctrine of friendship and good-will; of religious liberty and equal opportunity for all men of every nationality, color and creed.

After serving the City Mission, Morris Brown and Bethel in Phila., the time limit for work in one city came to an end, for at that time the Disciplinary limit for a pastorate in one city was four years.

During my first year at Bethel, the church debt referred to was paid, and the Sunday school attendance so increased that the Lecture room was over run, and we were obliged to put the body of the School in the main audience room, and the Infant Department in the galleries. It was a veritable army with banners, for we had class banners for the various classes and Departments, distributed all over the Church, and the sight was attractive and inspiring.

The popular and convenient hour for the holding of the Sunday school session was in the afternoon; say, from three to five o'clock. But, so long as the service was held in the Lecture room, an extra Church service would every now and then force its way to the main

andience room. This would naturally divide
the interest, and often the time also. For it
would frequently be necessary to abridge the
Sunday school service to permit the teachers
and others interested in the upstairs service
to be present. Such innovations made it difficult to build up a really first class Sunday
school, and was opposed by those who wanted
a model school, where the children would get
all the attention that they were entitled
to.

As to the pastor, he was often placed in
a dilemma. He was pastor of the Church, and
also chief superintendent of the Sunday school.
Both departments looked to him for aid and
decision whenever anything like controversy
came. It required thought and diplomacy to
satisfy the contending parties, and at the same
time avoid friction that would militate against
the best interests of the Church as a whole.
The best way to accomplish so delicate a task
as bringing harmony between the older and
younger elements of the Church, was to make
the Sunday school too large for the Lecture
Room, and thereby show the necessity of coming into the main audience room.

When this was accomplished to the satisfaction of all concerned, it was regarded by

Churchmen as a signal victory for the young and inexperienced pastor.

The meeting of the General Conference in 1880 brought about the usual changes in Episcopal Supervision. Bishop Payne was placed over the Second District, and Bishop John M. Brown over the First. Philadelphia was in the First and Baltimore was in the Second. Bethel Church, Philadelphia, and Bethel, Baltimore, were rivals. They were often referred to as twin sisters. It was a question, often discussed which was really established first. Daniel Coker was present at the 1816 Convention, representing the Baltimore Contingent of the movement to establish an independent Church. Bethel in Baltimore might claim equal right to the name of "Mother Church," and impose upon the historian the task of establishing the fact "beyond a reasonable doubt" that the Philadelphia building was erected first. But the fact that the meeting of 1816 that organized the African Methodist Episcopal Denomination was held at Bethel Church, Philadelphia, makes it defacto the Denominational Mother, while there can be no doubt about the claim of Bethel in Baltimore to the title of Mother African Methodist Church, South of Mason and Dixon

Line. Bishop Payne had a tender regard for the Baltimore charge. There he built the beautiful Church which building still stands as a storage room. Here he married his beloved "Julia:" his first marriage. Here his only child was born; the mother dieing in childbirth, and the child, a girl: "the refined and beautiful likeness of her mother," living a little over nine months. Here he had his longest and most successful pastorate, notwithstanding, a terrible Church fight in which blood was actually shed. He was victorious, however, and in after years, the people came to know and appreciate his real value as a Christian man, minister, and intelligent leader. The principal objection they had to him, and that which brought on the Church fight, was his opposition to the old form of sensational worship. Referring to the songs indulged in by those who took offense at his effort to bring about reform in worship, he characterized them as "corn-field ditties;" and, the swaying of the body and stamping of the feet, he called dancing.

In 1880, when he was sent to Baltimore as Bishop, the "Prayer-meeting Bands" were still in full force, and the "ditties" were not very unpopular with the minority who did not indulge in that form of worship, but tolerated it as a "necessary evil" in view of the fact that so many regarded it as an evidence of "spiritual life." I had one more year in Philadelphia, at Bethel, under Bishop John M. Brown to complete the full Disciplinary term of four years in one city. So soon as this was accomplished, Bishop Payne invited me to transfer to him to the Baltimore Conference, to which Bishop Brown consented. The Bishop did not intimate to me his purpose for having me transferred to his Conference, nor to what charge I was to be sent. But it turned out that I was to go to Bethel, and after the appointment, the Bishop intimated to me, what he expected me to do concerning certain reforms.

The afternoon service at Baltimore was a fixture. There had been a custom during long years for the "crowds" to go to the Sharp St. M. E. Church Sunday morning, and to Bethel Sunday afternoon.

One of Bethel's pastors got the reputation of driving the fastest horse on the Causeway, Sunday afternoon, after a wonderful sermon at Bethel Church.

When that master of Sunday school superintendents "Col." Isaac Myers made his advent

in Bethel and made that school the leading
school of the Denomination, the afternoon
Church service lost much of its popularity, but
still held its place. One of the things that
kept it alive was the custom of having an
itenerating or, changeable communion service;
that is, Communion was held every first Sunday in the month. alternately at the morning
afternoon and evening services. This service
being largely attended, it guaranteed a large
audience every third Sunday afternoon
whether or not. The Lecture Room was so
admirably adapted to the Sunday school work
that it was out of the question to move the
school from the Lecture Room, so, some
other excuse must be had for doing away with
the time-honored afternoon service. That the
older members generally wanted the service
whether they attended or not, and, that they
would not permit it to be set aside without a
struggle, or "rupture" as one expressed it, was
soon made known to the new preacher.

Diplomacy must again be resorted to, so
the pastor claimed that it was his indispensa-
ble duty to give attention to the Sunday
school service, and besides, he should as a
rule fill the pulpit morning and night and that

is all that should be expected or required of him.

There was a local preacher who was fond of preaching, he said of himself that he had a voice like Bishop Wayman, and that when you did not see the man in the pulpit, it was difficult to decide whether it was he or the Bishop. Here was an opportunity to put his eloquence to the test. So he was given the afternoon service as his very own, and was forbidden to invite any one else to take his place at any time. The service began to fall off, and finally fell out altogether.

About this time the Sunday School Union was organized permanently by Dr. C. S. Smith, and Children's Day established, the collections in Sunday school on which day was given to the support of the Union. Bethel Sunday School under the matchless management of "Col." Isaac Myers was the first to send a hundred dollars to the Union. It was secretary Smith—now Bishop Smith—who suggested the honorary title of Colonel for Mr. Myers.

During this administration, the M. E. Church on the corner of Linden Avenue and Garden St.—with two adjacent buildings—was purchased, and a new congregation organized, and the Church named Trinity. It became the leading A. M. E. Church in Baltimore, and only fell back to second place, when under the pastorate of the famous W. Sampson Brooks, Bethel Church came up again to first place.

Trinity Church was purchased at a cost of twenty-two thousand dollars, though there was not a member to begin the new society with nor a dollar to its credit. The purchase money was borrowed—$18,000—from Alexander Brown and Sons, bankers at Calvert and Baltimore Streets, thanks to the influence of "Colonel" Myers, with Bethel Church standing as security for the balance of $4000.

It was becoming evident to the man of vision, that Bethel could not remain indefinitely in Saratoga St., among the iron foundries and hold a leading place among the Churches. When Bethel was organized in the latter part of the eighteenth century, colored people sought a secluded spot for their Churches. In a back alley; behind the woods; where they could sing and pray late and loud without disturbing the "white folks." Bethel, down on the "marsh" was in a good place at first, but in 1881, times had changed, and were still changing rapidly.

I was offered forty-five thousand dollars

for the Saratoga street site, and an opportunity
to purchase the Presbyterian Church, parsonage and school house on the corner of Baltimore and Lord Sts. But when the meeting
was called, to consider the proposition, the
older members assembled enmasse, and if the
measure had been pushed, a riot might have
ensued. So, the project had to be given up.
When, however, the membership dwindled
down to a "hand full," and an attempt was
made to get out before all was lost, the old
historic spot sold for round about fifteen
thousand dollars.

It was some consolation, however, to return
in the course of years, as the presiding Bishop
of the District and lead the remnant out to
the present site, Druid Hill Ave., and Lanvale
St., and to see dear old Bethel, that was ready
to perish, restored to her pristine glory, the
leading Church among our people in the
Monumental City. Only a few remain to see
the people return from obscurity and reestab-
lish the temple. They were conspicuous by
their presence, and in their rejoicing at the
Brooks thirty-three thousand dollar rally June
16, 1919 Charley Dungee at the organ: Mrs.
Barnes on the choir: Mrs. Goldsboro, and Miss
Deaver among the forces that rolled up the

record breaking sum. Mrs. "Col." Myers at home waiting to hear the news. Mrs. Swan, feeble, unable to remain all night as the rest of us did. "Mamie" Handy, young in spirit, untiring in labor, liberal to a fault, and John Murphy, the Dean of Negro journalism sort of connecting link between the past and present. Messrs Hurst, Gaines, and Hill, expastors of the old Church on Saratoga St. Mr. and Mrs. Harris. A few others: some who went from the old Sunday school to Trinity, such as Florie Bennett. A nearly new congregation. The remnant that came up from old Bethel but do not belong to the '81 company, with the hundreds who have more recently joined the church, as new members or transfers from other congregations like Trinity, St. John, and Ebenezer make up the present membership; who, with friends from other denominations, it would seem indeed from all other denominations, and non-church members, won a victory unlike any financial accomplishment in the long and eventful history of the Church.

My pastorate in Baltimore embraced the years 1881-84, and closed with the General Conference which was held at Bethel. At this General Conference the A. M. E. Review had its birth with Dr. B. T. Tanner—after-wards Bishop Tanner—as its first editor. From this Conference, I returned with Bishop Cain to Philadelphia and by my own request was appointed to Allen Chapel. This was a small but self-sustaining Church, out of debt, and would offer me a long-sought opportunity to take a regular theological course, which I did at the P. E. Divinity School in West Philadel-phia. The requirement to enter as a regular student was a collegiate education or its equivalent. The six Professors, Drs. Bartlett, Myer-Smith, Garrison, Goodwin, Peters and Hare: taught respectively: Ecclesiastical His-tory: Homiletics and Pastoral Theology: Lit-turgics and Cannon Law: Apologetics—or Dogmatics—Hebrew and Greek. Hebrew was taught—if necessary—the first year. Greek must be acquired before entering. The course was New Testament Greek, and the penalty for bringing an English Bible into the Class room was expulsion from the school. The same was true of the Hebrew class room after the first year.

The course was in every way first class, and the professors represented even unusual scholarship. Dr. Peters graduate of Germany headed an archaeological exposition abroad. He and Dean Bartlett were joint authors of "The Church, Hebrew and Christian." Dr. Goodwin was an Ex-Dean of the University of Pennsylvania. Dr. Hare a vertible specialist in Greek was a member of the American Committee on the Revised version of the New Testament. Dr. Garrison gave up the practice of Medicine to take a chair in the school, and was an authority on Cannon Law. Dr. Myer-Smith, a practical preacher and pastor was at home on Homiletics and pastoral Theology. I entered the school in '84, and graduated in the class of '87. Besides the regular course, we had summer schools and lectures. The most important of the summer schools was that conducted by Prof. William R. Harper of the Chicago University, the universally acknowledged Hebrew specialist. His death which occured in the very prime of his life, and at the height of his usefulness, seemed indeed a calamity. He was as noble of spirit, as he was learned. With him, a student was a student; nothing more, and nothing less. He seemed totally incapable of that brand of race prejudice, based upon color, that so afflicts the average white American. It goes without saying that our school, under the Professors I have named, was free from this unchristian incubus, and the young men, students, who like myself, were preparing themselves to better represent the Master, as His ministers, regarded me simply as a fellow student. But for men and circumstances like these, we would sometimes be tempted like David once was, to say: "all men are liars." Those who come up to the Christian standard of brotherhood, regardless of prevailing traditions and standards, must be distinguished from those who claim to love God, but dispise a fellow being for no better reason than that by the accident of birth, he represents a different race variety.

I cannot estimate the value of three years of contact with these masters of assemblies. Their ripe experience; their profound scholarship; their plan of instruction, and their nobility of character, all combined to fit them, from any point of view, for the sacred task of teaching, directing and influencing men in their efforts to further prepare themselves for the work of the Christian ministry.

Having had about seven years of experience in ministerial work, I was all the more prepared to take in and appreciate the course that I was now taking. With me, it was a combination of theory and practice. As a pastor even then, I could apply in a practical way the lessons and experiences that came day by day.

One of the Summer Schools attended immediately after the completion of the Divinity School course, was one by Professor Gould, in New Testament Greek. We took up the Book of Revelation for sight reading, exegesis and interpretation. Before this, Revelation—this Book of figures and symbols—had always remained a mystery to me. After that, in preparing a simple work called "Key to Scriptural Interpretations," I was bold enough to make the Revelation one of the chapters.

To whatever extent I shall always be aware of my limitations, I shall always regard the course at the Divinity School, as contributing largely to the measure of preparedness, that by dint of severe discipline and application, both in and out of school, I was able to acquire.

At the General Conference that met at Indianapolis in 1888, I was elected Editor of the A. M. E. Church Review, to succeed Dr. Tanner, who was elected Bishop at that meeting.

Journalism! Surely it requires some courage for a venture like this. Of course there are Editors, and editors; Journalists and journalists.

Our weekly and monthly periodicals in the form of newspapers had begun to multiply, but previous to the advent of the periodical in question, no one among us had undertaken to put on the market a Quarterly Review. Rather pretentious title! Some of the church leaders were in favor of launching a magazine instead of a Review. A magazine would consist of articles upon various subjects; but, a Review would be this and more, and to make such a periodical fill its mission with credit, would require a high degree of literary ability: experience would come in time.

But Dr. B. T. Tanner, who had the reputation of being our very best editor, was willing to undertake the publication of such a literary journal, and the ability with which he edited and published it, proved that he made no mistake in undertaking so exacting a task.

As the succesor of Dr. Tanner I had his confidence, sympathy and co-operation. Magazine and Review writers are paid for their articles. Some of them command large sums for their productions. But the A. M. E. Review had no funds with which to pay for articles. True our object was to confine the articles almost exclusively to colored writers, as they, more than others needed the opportunity that the Review would offer; moreover, it was a race enterprise. But our best writers were beginning to get into the Reviews and magazines, and get pay for their articles, and it was the best writers that we wanted, and needed to give character to our publication.

Bishop Tanner was acquainted with the literary men among us, he being of the same craft, and they generally sympathized with the movement, so the difficulty in obtaining articles without pay was not insuperable. There was this advantage, our own church members, ministerial and lay, could be depended upon to have sufficient interest in the enterprise to contribute their articles gratuitously. Then, some who aspired to be magazine writers could expect to be given an opportunity for their products that they might not be able to get in the older productions.

Volume I, July '84, opens with Bishop D. A. Payne as first contributor. Then Bishops Campbell, Dickerson, Ward and Turner follow. Other contributors are: Mrs. F. E. W. Harper; Judge D. Augustus Straker, Prof. W. S. Scarboro, Hon. B. K. Bruce, Rev. J. H. Durant, Rev. William H. Thomas and Dr. T. G. Steward. These contributions, with the

Editor's trenchant pen, constituted the first number of this new venture.

I was fortunte enough to keep the old friends of the Review and to make new ones. I could always depend upon my old friends, T. Thomas Fortune and T. McCants Stuart to come to my rescue, as I could also Judge Straker. Every now and then I would have an article from Prof. Orishatuka Faduma, of West Africa; and the Hon. Frederick Douglass frequently contributed. But those ·here mentioned are but a small number of those who contributed between the years of 1884, when the Review began, and 1896, when my mission as Editor closed.

The reviews of the work given from time to time by the literary journals that we exchanged with were sometimes very favorable; even flatteringly so. Of course, we came in also for our share of adverse criticism.

Rev. George Brent wrote an article on "The Origin of the White Man," and proved by the Bible, apparently to his own satisfaction, that Gehazi, the servant of Elisha, who deceived his master, and ran after Naaman and took gifts for his healing by the prophet, was the true progenitor of the white race. See II Kings 4th chapter.

This conclusion was ridiculed by one of the leading Reviews, and the Editor was severely censured for permitting such to be published.

A gentleman, who is an artist of more or less distinction, got an idea that he was also a poet, seeming to forget that "poets are born." So he sent in a poem. It had a rather unique title; was clothed in fairly dazzling English, conveying in rather an abstract manner what seemed to have been some indefinite ideas in his mind that were struggling more for classification than for utterance. The production was displayed in most beautiful penmanship, on spotless paper. The workmanship was really a thing of beauty, fully sustaining the reputation of the author's ability to handle a pen, or brush. But as a poem, I could not find the subject, nor where it began or ended. If I could have just had the manuscript bound as a part of the Review, the printed matter would have certainly suffered in comparison for artistic finish; but of course this could not be done. After considerable hesitance, I decided to print it, and share with the author the consequences. One of the leading exchanges, after referring to the fact that the A. M. E. Review was out, with quite an array of articles upon different subjects, which made it quite an interesting number, called special attention to the poem in question, and said: "the man who wrote that poetry cannot escape punishment; for it will surely be meted out to him, either in this world or the world to come."

The selecting of articles for the Review was no easy task. Our main support—financial support—was not from the most scholarly class, and it often happened that one who had not gained a reputation as a writer would send in an article, and feel that on account of the material support given by himself and his friends, it should appear. This was especially true of ministers connected with our conferences. They began to say: "We support the Review, and we want to be given a place in its columns."

Bishop T. M. D. Ward often referred to the Review as "the cream jug of the Connection." At one of his conferences he discovered that one of the ministers was having a parley with the Editor. The Bishop was hard of hearing, and could not make out what the conversation was about, but he suspected that the Editor had met with objections when asking for a subscription. "What is the trouble there," asked the Bishop, his mouth twitching with a characteristically humorous smile. "He was asking me to take the Review," responded the minister. "It is one dollar and a half," said the Bishop. "But I do not care to take it," replied the minister. "One dollar and a half" said the Bishop again. "But, suppose I haven't got the money," said the minister. The Bishop leaning forward, said again. "One dollar and a half." Upon this, the contending party took the amount from his pocket and entered the list of subscribers.

The position of editor of a literary journal puts one in touch with the literati of his day, and brings to him many books for review. Besides, it forces one to endeavor to keep abreast of the times, for he is expected to know something of all that is going on. This is one position in the Church that does not have a large number of aspirants. Men will aspire to the Bishopric who would not at all be taken seriously should they run for editorship of the Review. The more the pity! When men do not know what they are fitted for, those whose suffrage they ask should assist them in finding out. This should not only be true of one who might at an unguarded moment ask for a literary place that he was incapable of filling, but much more concerning one who, without the Pauline standard of qualification comes forward and unblushingly asks for the most sacred position in the gift of the Church: one that rightly demands the highest intelligence, and the strictest conformity to the demands of morality and religion.

My term as Editor was from May, 1888, to to May, 1896, eight years.

At the General Conference of 1896, which met at Wilmington, N. C., either by the strong solicitation of friends, or by a strong personal desire for the place, perhaps both, I was a candidate for the Bishopric. The laymen of the Church supported me loyally, but with the understanding that if I failed of election, one of their number, namely, Prof. H. T. Keeling, would be my successor. I failed of election, and Professor Keeling accordingly was elected in my stead.

My membership as a minister was in the Philadelphia Conference. The conference met immediately after the rise of the General Conference. I took my place in the ranks and was appointed by Bishop A. Grant to the pastorate of "Mother Bethel." This, then, was my second term as pastor of Bethel. My first term was two years, the second, four, six in all, and the longest pastorate at this church since its pastor—Bishop Richard Allen. Other pastors, like myself, have been returned, but remained two years at each term.

Rev. C. T. Shaffer had built a new church on the old spot, and there remained a considerable indebtedness. Already the membership had begun to go with the city trend, west, and southwest, and the attendance was not what it was when I occupied the pulpit before.

My first effort was to increase the attendance and organize a financial rally that would net a larger sum of money than the average rally produced. When the rally day came I had the presence of my Bishop, and also of Dr. John W. Beckett, of most precious memory.

The day was fair; the attendance large; enthusiasm high, and the amount realized was thirty-two hundred dollars. This was before the days of Drs. Carl M. Tanner with his sixteen thousand, and W. Sampson Brooks, with his thirty-theee thousand, and was, I think, about the largest amount, up to that time, raised in one day by any one of our churches.

The second pastorate at Bethel was with greatly added experience, and compared with

the first, was entitled to be in every way
stronger. Age and experience count for much
in the ministry, as well as in other vocations.
To be called to the work, and to be spiritually
strong are first and most in ministerial preparedness, but not all. Nothing can take the
place of experience.

Sixteen years had passed since I first pastored Bethel. I had seen much of men and
things. I had traveled at large over the larger
part of the United States. I had gone from
Atlantic City, in the East, to San Francisco, in
the West, and besides visited all of the Southern States where our people are in hundreds
of thousands and many hundred thousands. I
had come into personal and intimate contact
with race leaders North, South and West. I
had seen my people at their homes; in their
churches; on their farms; in business and professional life, and in every grade of society.. I
had seen them at their best and at their worst.
I had been permitted to study them at close
range and at leisure. I had not simply ridden
on cars through state after state, stopping
here and there, and spending a night; but I
had been with them day and night, living and
moving and having my being among them.
This in itself is a great education, and one

that cannot be acquired in schools. In my great desire in former years to prepare myself, by every possible means for my life's work, I had no thought that there was in store for me so great a privilege for education by travel and contact as the editorship of the Review afforded.

I began with my advent upon the Review, to acquire a library. I had collected some books; school books, theological works, and a few of a miscellaneous character. But now I thought of building up a large and varied libary of current and standard works.

Abaham Lincoln once said: "Books have what I want." The Angel said to John: "What thou seest, write in a book." Books are the records of what men have seen and learned and believed, and proved, since the world began. Books have what we need for instruction, for investigation and enlightenment. Books do not forget, or change. Once a matter is recorded with printer's ink it remains unchanged. They are a storehouse of knowledge from which we can draw upon all subjects. Of course there are books and books, so care should be had in selecting a library. Some books are beautifully bound in loud and attractive colors, and put into cases, to adorn

a library. These, as a rule, are never read.
Then there are tons of books put on the market that are not worth reading. To read them
would be but a waste of time and energy.
What we need is good books. A well selected
libary is invaluable, and necessary. A young
man called on me at my home in Philadelphia,
saying he was engaged in a joint debate upon
a subject upon which he was seeking information, and requested me to refer him to a
public library where there might be a chance
of finding what he neened. I told him I
thought I knew of such a library, and invited
him to my study. After spending some time
there he decided that it was unnecessary to go
further in quest of the information he wanted.
A well furnished library should so represent
what popularly comes under the head of "Art,
Science and Literature" that one might be
able to find in it something on any subject desired.

Good books are in demand, and are costly,
and besides requiring time to select a good
working library, it requires also considerable
money to purchase it. But it is a paying in-
vestment for the literary, the professional
man who wants to do his best work.

I did not purchase a commentary on the

Bible until I had been preaching quite a dozen years, then I bought the Pulpit Commentary, and it is the only one I have ever possessed. One should not substitute books for brains, nor become a slave to the thoughts and conclusions of others. This is especially true where conscience has or should have much to do with final decisions. I consider the Dictionary of the Bible, edited by James Hastings, M.A., D.D., a valuable asset to a minister's library. In spite of my care in selecting I find myself with several encyclopaedias, and cyclopaedias; literary, historical, biographical. I prize Lord's "Beacon Lights" and "Stoddardt's Lectures" and Charles Dickens' Works. There are many standard works that seem necessary to a complete library. Beware of the "Who is Who?" agents that come around occasionally to convince you that you are one of the who's. I once said to Bishop Arnett, after I had read a book entitled "Men of Mark," that I found some men in it who, so far as I knew, were not very remarkable. The Bishop replied: "The author of the book simply said men of mark, without indicating whether it was to be a big mark or a little one."

I have a section in my library that I call "Black Boys." These are all books by colored authors. Of course the Paul Laurence Dunbar library is among the collection. I was greatly assisted by the late Carl Boliver, in making this collection of colored authors, as I was originally inspired to do so by the late Bishop B. W. Arnett, who is author of the name: "Black Boys."

In this collection I have an old and rare volume—out of print of course—called: "The Rise and Progress of the Kingdoms of Light and Darkness, or the Reign of Kings Alpha an Abadon," by Lorenzo D. Blackson. Published in 1867. It is a counterpart of the "Pilgrims' Progress," and it is written in exactly the same style, poetry and all.

The author was a minister in the U. A. M. E. Church, known also as the Peter Spencer Church, whose founder was present at the 1816 meeting at Philadelphia when the A. M. E. Church was organized. History says that Spencer did not go with Allen in his movement, because he opposed the intineracy. His preachers would work in the field all the week and preach on Sunday, sometimes after walking many miles, and only receive the few pennies that would be thrown into the collection basket. They were encouraged to be very "spiritual," with the idea that "the letter killeth, but the spirit maketh alive." I often heard them preach during my residence in Wilmington, Del., the original home of Father Spencer, and his Church. There were among them some very talented men, such as the father of Rev. Solomon Porter Hood, of the A. M. E. Church. The Senior Hood would be an able preacher in the present day. He was a giant in stature. When he walked into the pulpit, and the steps creaked under his feet, some one in the audience would shout: "Amen." He was intelligent and able; not learned, as is his son, who has had the advantage of freedom and the schools. Well, our subject, Lorenzo Dow Blackson, like Reverend Hood, was about the average in intelligence, though, unlike Reverend Hood, he was not a great preacher. He finally sought a more congenial field and died in the A. M. E. Zion Church. He believed in "entire sanctification" and preached it. What is more, lived it. He could sustain himself in an argument ment upon the doctrine he preached. After preaching fifty years he was active; still writing and preaching. I believe that if the book should be republished, the scholars and churchmen of the present day would discover its true value as the men of his day did not.

I was invited to be the principal speaker at his funeral, which I considered an honor.

We are beginning now to produce authors whose writings will go upon the shelves of public libraries, and in the homes of literary men and women regardless of race variety.

When our authors and editors of marked ability get a hearing before the world, public opinion will undergo a change, because the merits and virtues of the "brother in black" will be set forth as well as his demerits and so-called backwardness.

My library is my constant companion: men and women with whom I can converse, and with whom I cannot be lonesome. The Bible and the other books.

CHAPTER. VII.

Across the Continent.

Many people who go abroad sight seeing, are embarrased when questioned about the Niagara Falls, Pikes Peake, and scenes in California, if obliged to confess that they have never seen them. A foreigner once said to such a person: "Why do you not go travelling in your own country, before going abroad?"

As Editor of the A. M. E. Review I had an opportunity to travel quite a good deal. I had been to all of the New England States, the middle States, the Southern States, and as far West as Wisconsin, but had not crossed the Continent, from Ocean to Ocean. So I resolved to make the journey. Having done so, I wrote an editorial on the trip. Such journeys may happen once in a lifetime: but with most people they never happen. Again it may be that only a few Review subscribers have preserved all the numbers.

With a view of putting it in permanent form I herewith submit the editorial, "ACROSS THE CONTINENT."

During the first four years as editor of the REVIEW, we were unable to visit the coast of California, and thus make a circuit of our home fields. Only once in the history of our Church had a general officer visited the Far West. Believing that such a visit would be good, both for the work by encouraging the workman, and also for the editor, by broadening his experience, we resolved to go.

Accordingly, on Friday, July 21st, 1893, we left the office work in the hands of our good friend, Rev. J. Albert Johnson, and boarding a train on the Pennsylvania Road, started "West". Our always pleasant friend and associate editor, Rev. H. T. Johnson—of the Christian Recorder—accompanied us as far as Chicago, where he was going to attend the meeting of "Educators." We spent several days in the "White City." The great Columbian Fair was in full blast. Great and marvelous are the exhibits of art, science and natural products. Who can do more than faintly describe them?

Perhaps no city in the Union is so eminently prepared to hold such a big Fair as this

Queen City of the West. The Bureau of Public Comfort announced its ability to feed
60,000 persons per hour within the Exhibition
grounds, and the hotels and boarding houses
of the city were prepared to accomodate hundreds of thousands. Early in the season it
became evident to the management that ex-
orbitant prices would not pay. The railroads
were a little stubborn, and insisted on keeping
up rates, and in some cases they put on a
"Fast Columbian Express" and charged extra.
The traveling public was not long in deciding
that between high rates of travel and of ac-
comodation at the city, a trip there would be
too expensive for the average pocketbook. As
soon as the managers of the Fair and the railroad managers began to reduce rates the attendance began to increase, and, at this writing
there is hope that the affair will be a financial
success. The Sunday opening question gave
trouble from the very beginning, and although
the managers insisted upon opening on Sunday in defiance of the expressed conditions
upon which they received national aid, they
were unable to make it popular. Many Exhibits were closed on Sunday, thus making it
impossible for those who visited only on Sundays to see all that was to be seen.

When we first entered the grounds—via Midway Plaisance—we decided that several days would be required to simply walk through the grounds, to say nothing of anything like a critical inspection of all the buildings. The various attractions of the Plaisance were quite enough to occupy several days.

Some of the attractions along the avenue were the Diamond Match company; Model Workman's Home; International Costume Exhibit, with about fifty living representatives of different nationalities, races and types, each clad in native costume; Nursery Exhibit; Electrice Scenic Theatre; Libby Glass company; Japanese Bazaar; Japanese Village; German Village; Lecture Hall, illustrating the science of animal locomotion; Persian Palace; Eiffel Tower, Street in Cairo; Ferris Wheel, revolving 250 feet in the air; East India Bazaar; Algernian and Tunisian Village; Kilanea Panorama, showing the noted Hawaiian Volcano; Chinese Village; Brazil Concert Hall; National Hungarian Orpheum; Lapland Villiage; Dahomey Village; Old Vienna; St. Peter's Model; Glass Spinning House; Ice Railway; Moorish Palace, Turkish Village; Cyclorama of Berniee Alps; South Sea Islanders; Hogenbeck's Animal Show; Venice-Murano company

glass exhibit,; Log Cabin; Nursery; Blarney
Castle and Irish Village. The admission to
those various attractions on Midway Plaisance varies from 10 to 50 cents. It costs from
$12 to $15 to visit them all, and would require
nearly a week. Now, when one remembers
that this is but the entrance to the Fair and
not really the Fair proper, he can get an idea
of its immense proportions. It would be useless to attempt a description of the various
exhibits, suffice it to name the general departments, which are as follows: Agricultural,
Horticultural, Live Stock, Fish, Mining, Machinery, Transportation; Manufactures, Elec-
tricity, Fine Arts, Liberal Arts, and Ethnology.

In those various General Departments,
twelve in number, are exhibited the various
products of nature under cultivation, and of
human genius and skill. Almost every civilized
nation is represented with exhibits giving an
idea of its wealth in natural resources and of
inventive genius.

There were two exhibits that we were
especially anxious to see, and to which we
hastened, and these were the exhibits of Wilberforce University and the Haitian Building.

The exhibit of Wilberforce was small, compared with some other institutions, and es-

pecially some of the exhibits of the Roman
Catholic Church; and the Haitian building was
humble compared with many of the massive
structures that surrounded it and overshadowed it; but Wilberforce and Haiti represented
a people, the genius, industry, and capability
of whom, but for them, would have been without representation, or, as is frequently the case
would have been misrepresented.

The genius of the Negro is interwoven with
the civilization of America, and indeed of the
world, but in such a way as to leave him without credit. Hence the burning question, can
the descendants of Ham do anything great?
Or, must it be left alone to Shem and Japhet
to show the trend of progress under a higher
civilization? Wilberforce and Haiti answered
at the World's Fair—Wilberforce with her
institutions of learning, organized and managed from begining to end by colored men, and
Haiti with her Republic, whose independence
was gained by her brave and noble Toussaint
L'Ouverture, and maintained by his successors,
Our thanks are due to Bishop B. W. Arnett
and the Hon. Frederick Douglass for getting
the Negro before the assembled nations in
other than a subordinate relation.

We divided our time during the week of our

stay between sightseeing at the Exposition grounds and the Educational Congress, which held its meetings at the Liberal Arts Building, foot of Adams Street. The meetings were really good, as could only have been the case, since they were participated in by some of the first educators of the world. The part contributed by colored educators was altogether creditable. Strong papers were read by many on various subjects, and stirring addresses were made by others. A special point of interest brought to light by these meetings was the fact that a goodly number of colored teachers are teaching in public or mixed schools. Many of our people opposed mixed schools, because they feared that it would deprive our teachers of their positions. Many of us believed that while this would be the case at first, that even this difficulty would be overcome as our teachers made themselves indispensible. Statistics upon the subject, given by delegates, show that colored teachers at work in public schools are as follows: Massachusetts, 14; Michigan, 5; Ohio, 11; Pennsylvania, 2; Minnesota, 3; New York, 2; Illinois, 2. Thirty-nine in all. This does not include those who are required to do normal work before leaving College. These statistics tell their own story of the progress that we are making.

The Chicago Fair demonstrates in a high degree the capability of man. When he began to inhabit the earth it was in a very crude state, but he was commanded by his creator to take possession of his territory and subdue it. The march of civilization, as it is exhibited by the Columbian Fair, shows how well man has been doing his work. The rivers and mountains are no longer barriers to his onward march, but are made his servants. By an enlightened mind directing the skilled hand, he has invented all manner of machinery, by which the burdens of life are greatly lifted, labor is dignified and time is saved. The four quarters of the globe are brought together and all nations of the earth are made neighbors. But as the thoughtful man looks upon these wonderful acheivements with admiration, he is forcibly reminded of two things—first, that these great accomplishments are the result of years and centuries of study, toil, and sacrifice. We stand, looking upon a mass of machinery, with its thousand different parts curiously wrought, skillfully put together and set in motion, and we say great are the wisdom and skill of the inventor. But upon a sober second thought we remember that all those mighty works in art had humble beginnings. the teakettle is mother of the gigantic steam engine that is capable of running a mile in thirty seconds. The costly fabric in tapestry and fine linen sprang from the fig leaf apron. From the dirt-made hut has sprung the hall, the place of marvelous acheivements in architectural skill. The first plow to break the soil for the husbandman was a sharpened stick, but now the art of tilling the soil has risen to such dignity that the Department of Agriculture is the first to be named on the official guide at the World's Columbian Exposition. The lesson to be learned by these progressive steps in civilization is that any nation or any race variety that would rise to the degree of excellence attained by those that are now on exhibition at the "White City" must be industrious and patient. There is a philosophy in progress, and this must be regarded by all who would compete with progressive nations.

But, again, the thoughtful observer is reminded that the great accomplishments before him are the results of Christian civilization. How many kingdoms have risen and fallen, and how many exalted nations have been brought low because they did not recognize the claim

of Him whose right it is to rule. Most all the
nations represented at the Columbian Exposition are Christian nations, and those that are
not are perceptibly behind in the procession.
China, the oldest civilization that is represented here, is but an infant compared with
England, France, Germany and America. These
nations as representatives of Christianity, have
their imperfections, and for these we neither
praise nor excuse them; upon the face of the
sun there are spots, yet he outshines the
moon.

At the expiration of another century, when
all the civilized nations assemble to take account of their acheivements, what nation will
be first in the sisterhood? May we not give
the answer of our Lord when he was asked
who shall be greatest in the kingdom of heaven?

Leaving Chicago, our next stop was Denver,
Col. Some one has spoken thus eloquently of
Denver:

"Poets have poured forth their souls in the
marvelous measures of rhythmic rhapsody;
artists have felt their deft fingers tingle and
thrill while they painted the never ending
glories of peaks and plain; historians, statis-

ticians and scientists have struggled together in a vain effort to comprehend the possibilities of a region unlike anything ever before heard of in song or story or the cheerless realm of hard dry facts and figures. They had seen Colorado, they were wrestling with a stupendous problem—the destiny of Denver. There is only one Denver. There never has been, there never can be another, for there is no influence which can create its equal."

The writer was evidently speaking of the Denver of the past, and what we trust will also be the Denver of the future, for upon our arrival we found fourteen banks suspended, and a city fairly wearing the badge of mourning. Neither Denver as a city, nor Colorado as a State can prosper with closed mines. The depreciation of silver closed· all the mines at Leadville, and shut went the banks of Denver. Colorado's output of bullion—gold, silver, lead and copper—for the year 1892, aggregated in value $37,017,993. This enormous product came principly to the smelters of Denver. Agriculture, horticulture, manufacturing, and other interests and industries have helped Denver, but the mining interests made it chiefly, and without this interest it must remain badly crippled. Since the great money panic

began, real estate in Denver has depreciated
more than 50 per cent.

Our church work in this metropolitan city
has for four years been in the hands of that
king of financiers, Rev. P. A. Hubbard. The
bonded debt when he took the church was
$8,000. He went to work with a determina-
tion to reduce the indebtedness by at least
$2,000 each year. Though the membership is
less than 300, he succeeded in carrying out his
plans, and just before the panic came had paid
the last dollar. During the years when he was
constantly urging the necessity of paying the
entire debt, many thought him too exacting,
and saw no good reason why the entire debt
should be paid, so long as the interest was kept
up. But he could not be persuaded to relax
his efforts, and now that they have made their
escape from the great financial depression that
is upon us, every one is loud in the praise of P.
A. Hubbard. But this long and constant strain
told on his health, and he was glad to join us
and go out to the "Coast" seeking a renewal
of health.

Another thing that the good people of Denver, with their heroic pastor, must be given
credit for, is that in managing the heavy work
of their own church they were not forgetful

of the needs of others; so they planted two missions, one in the western and the other in the northern portions of the city. These missions are pastored by two faithful young men, Revs. James Smith and Robert Cason. The old church—Shorter Chapel—has nourished them as a mother would a child.

The pastors and people of these missions regret much that the time of Rev. Hubbard has expired. The disciplinary limit moves him. But we must trust in the goodness of God and the wisdom of the Bishop to send a faithful successor of him who has worked so faithfully and successfully at this post for four years. Of course he cannot be returned. We must keep our rules, "not for wrath, but for conscience sake."

At Denver, Col., we met Mr. Leroy Hayes, who gave some very interesting statistics of our people who have left the South and gone West. Mr. Hayes lived at No. 2229 Arapaho Street. Through his efforts, and by the aid of the Union Pacific, 3,090 persons have been brought out during the last three years and located as follows: Idaho, 800; Washington, 900; California. 650; Colorado, 480; Utah 260. These for the most part have been settled on farms; 110 families have been settled in Kehrn

County, California; 360 persons have been put
to work in the Rouse Mines. The 800 that
were left in Idaho were given free transportation from Texas; 800 of the 900 that were
carried to Washington are operating mines

In San Joaquin County, California, a tract
of 3,000 acres of land has been taken up by
those who have come out in search of better
homes. We have observed that colored set-
tlers, especially in California, are being encouraged, while the Chinese are not in good
favor. This is probably because the Chinese
do not take kindly to our civilization. Rev.
C. B. Caldwell, one of our pastors in Tennessee,
came out some months ago, and procured several thousand acres of excellent land in Salt
Lake Valley, upon which he expected to settle a colony.

Mr. Hayes said to me in an interview: "I
have now a proposition on hand providing that
if we can secure one hundred families, farmers, an Eastern syndicate will set apart 360
acres as a town site in a Southern Colorado
farming district, erect a town hall, and furnish
employment, in the laying out of streets,
building the town hall, and other public buildings, for at least one hundred and fifty men,
for three months prior to the coming of the

colony. The syndicate further agrees to sup-
ply water by ditch right to the farming district, with the privilege of the persons purchasing farm tracts and paying for them by
working on the ditch and laterals; provided,
however, 80 percent of the required number
purchase farm tracts of 80 acres each, not to
exceed in the purchase price $26.00 per acre
with water rights. The remaining 20 per cent
to controll the stores of the city. I have con-
tracts similar to this for Colorado, Utah, California and New Mexico." Mr. Hayes further
said that the mistake made by many who
have come out is that they settle in the cities
instead of taking up the farm lands. Said he:
"We are not looking for loafers, but for men
who are willing to go out on farms and work
and such will not only be welcomed, but will
receive encouragement and substantial help."

Mr. Hayes and Mr. J. C. Watson have been
very active in assisting our people who desire
to go West, settle lands and better their condition. Mr. Hayes has promised to give us
such information from time to time as will
be of interest to home seekers in this portion
of our country. The columns of the REVIEW
are always open to such information. We do
not discourage African Emigration. Our peo-

ple have as good right to go to Africa as any
other people, but they also have as good right
to possess themselves of the unsettled lands of
the West as has any other people. To wait
until the wild lands have been brought under
cultivation, and cities are built by others, then
go, is to submit to subordinate relation among
the people of the rich and vigorous West, and
to enjoy no more real independence there than
we enjoy in the East and South.

If we have not courage sufficient to do pioneer work in the land of our nativity, we would
not be very valuable accessions to the undeveloped Continent of Africa.

But we must continue our journey. Leaving
Denver, Col., the next point of interest to
which the attention of the tourist is called is
Palmer Lake. But few passengers stop here
longer than is necessary to get lunch. It is
scarcely necessary to say any more about this
station than that it has a population of about
200, is fifty two miles from Denver; the elevation is 7,237 feet, and is said to be a very
healthy place. There is a curious fact, however, about Palmer Lake, it is situated exactly
upon the summit of an arm of the Rockies,
called the "Divide." From the crest of this
summit the waters divide, flowing northward

into the Platte, and southward into the Arkansas, as it "wends its way into the Mississippi."

Those who remain here will find much to engage them in visiting points of interest in the vicinity. But our party pushed on to Colorado and Manitou Springs. These two cities are twins, they are coupled together both by steam and electric car roads. Colorado Springs has a population of 10,000, and does not allow a drop of intoxicating liquors of any kind sold there. Every deed that is executed contains this prohibitory condition. A large number of millionaires live here. They have made the city what it is as a residence city and health resort, and they do not intend to have their quiet disturbed by intoxicated persons. Indeed the city ordinance even forbids the ringing of a bell, except it be a fire bell; hence the church goers must watch the time on Sundays as well as on other days. We have an interesting church work at this point. The building is of Colorado stone, and is situated on the corner of two broad avenues. The congregation is wide awake, and thinks much of its rank in the Colorado Conference. The population of Manitou is 1,000. This place is, in our opinion, the finest health resort in our great Western world. It is situated at the foot of Pikes

Peak, and has the famous effervescent soda
and iron springs. Visitors are permitted to
drink all the mineral water they desire and to
carry away at each visit a quart of the health-
giving draught. At each spring a boy is stationed with a large ladle, and he courteously
waits on all who come either for a drink or
for a quart allowance.

The attractions near the Manitou, varying
from one to seven miles, are; Manitou Grand
Caverns, Cave of the Winds, Ute Pass, and
Rainbow Falls, Red Canyon, Crystal Park, Garden of the Gods, Glen Eyerie, Monument Park,
Seven lakes, North Cheyenne Canyon, and pos-
sibly the most famous of all, Summit of Pike's
Peak. The height of Pike's Peak is 14,147
feet, and is never entirely clear of snow. Three
members of the United States Signal Service
Corps live on the Peak continually. There is
a cog railway line that carries passengers up
daily at a cost of $2.50 per round trip; the
fare has been as much as $5.00. Off to the left
of the iron spring, situated at a considerable
height, are two prominent rocks called "Gog
and Magog." We do not promise that the
visitor to them will get any light thrown upon
the rather mysterious passage in the "Revelation" bearing these names, but we can as-

sure him that he will have a tedious journey and will be surrounded by that which is grand and beautiful in nature.

Nestling upon the hill-sides on every hand and at the base of the mountains, are residences of unique design; some are private and others are boarding houses for the accommodation of those who come seeking pleasure, recreation and health.

And now onward to Pueblo, which someone has called "the Pittsburg of the West," not at all counting Pittsburg as a western city. The population of this city is 25,000, and they are an interprising set. This, at least, is the reputation that it bears. Our party did not stop here, but we were met at the train by our able and enterprising pastor, Rev. S. W. Byrd, who seemed to anticipate the appetizing effect that the mountain air would have upon us, and so he brought a large basket full of food prepared especially for the occasion. It is needless to say that we enjoyed the repast, and that elder Byrd deserves and has our most hearty thanks. I might as well say now that our company consisted of Bishop and Mrs. Handy; Rev. P. A. Hubbard, wife and daughter; Mrs. Fanny J. Coppin and the editor of the REVIEW. The bishop, of course, was

at the head of the company. Brother Hubbard was general manager and we gladly acknowledge his efficiency as such. The ladies
were the indispensibles to the comfort and the
happiness of the party, and it remained for
the REVIEW man to gather a few items for
publication. On our return from the coast
the Bishop and wife stopped at Pueblo, and he
reports the church-work here as being in good
condition. We have one church and parsonage at this point and an active membership.

The run over the Denver and Rio Grande, between Pueblo and Leadville, may be called
the scenic portion of this route. The natural
beauty of the country is in many instances
simply beyond description. The train halts
at Canyon City, which is a point of considerable interest, a health and pleasure resort, and
a business center. But the name reminds the
traveller that he is soon to enter that grand
conyon of the Arkansas, the narrowest portion of which is known as the Royal Gorge.
Here nature and art meet, and fairly vie with
each other in stupendous work of beauty and
wonder. The daring civil engineer has followed the river in its manderings, and con-
tended with cliff and boulder until he has made
a roadbed for his train. Such an accomplish-

ment seems at a glance to be impossible; it
is only the stubborn fact that the road bed
is actually there that compels one to acknowledge the possibility of such a feat. All passengers are at the windows and open the
platform, if not in the observation car—when
this Gorge is entered. Lower and lower the
train seems to sink, while the dashing, foam-
ing river rushes by in wild fury. Higher and
higher the almost perpendicular mountains
rise, until the highest peak looks down from
a distance of three thousand feet upon the
train below as it cautiously carries its precious cargo. There comes over one a feeling
akin to reverential awe as he passes through
this wonderful path chiseled out by the hand
of nature; as he views the granite cliffs upon
which tree or shrub never grows, and up which
even the aboriginal grizzly cannot climb. With
silence or with abated voice the traveller passes through this wonderful scene.

Leaving the grand canyon, our next important stop was Leadville. If there are a
people in the great West who are nothing
wanting in their ability to entertain strangers,
they are found at Leadville. Representatives
of the Methodist Episcopal and Baptist churches—white—turned out with our people   to

welcome and entertain us. Father Rice holds
the fort at this point. He is an old pioneer
workman out here, and all delight to do him
honor. But "how doth the city lie desolate
that was full of people!" On our arrival here
the city was fairly wearing the badge of
mourning. The depreciation of the value of
silver had closed the mines and smelters. It
is to be remembered that Leadville is the richest mining district in the state of Colorado.

It was Leadville that made Denver the
great rich city that it is. Lead, silver and
iron are its chief products. When we are informed that in less than twelve months this
place rose from a small hamlet of less than
fifty inhabitants to a city of thirty-five thous-
and population, we can easily imagine the
wealth of the mines that drew so many fortune seekers. The total value of Leadville
smelting industry for 1892 is given at $11,509,-
643.37. When silver went down and the mines
and smelters closed, three thousand men were
put out of work who had been averaging three
dollars per day. The people out here are in-
tense bimetalists, and if there is but one metal used as a legal tender, they prefer the white
metal. When we were asked for our opinion
upon the silver question, we referred them to

the REVIEW for July, 1893, in which is Mr. Fortune's able article on "Free Coinage."

The West, Colorado especially, will suffer greatly if the momentary condition of the country remains much longer as it is—August 25th, 1893. But we have good hope that the extraordinary session of Congress will bring relief. Bimetalism seems to us the only solution. We need gold, silver and paper to do the commercial business of this country, and of the world, and any attempt to lessen the volume is sure to give trouble. The South and West evidently knew previous to the last national election that their chosen standard bearer was not in sympathy with the financial plank of the platform promulgated at the Chicago Convention. But if it were of doubtful interpretation then, it is evident now that the Democratic Party is a house divided against itself.

The next point of interest to mention after leaving Leadville, is Salt Lake City. Of this historic city and the mystic Salt Lake, our readers have had a description in a previous number of the REVIEW. Suffice it to say that Salt Lake City was founded by Brigham Young, the great Mormon leader who went out to Utah in 1847, and that it now ranks

among the first class cities of the far West.
When application was made to the United
States to make the territory of Utah a State,
the people found that a barrier stood in their
way, and that was the practice of plural marriages, which seems to be the principal thing
in the religion of "the Latter Day Saints," as
the Mormons are wont to call themselves.
They are now forbidden by the United States
to celebrate any more plural marriages. This
prohibition was almost a death blow to the
Mormon church at this place, and the result
is that many are seeking other quarters. Nevertheless, they are still a strong and important element in Salt Lake City. The Temple
that was begun in 1853 was finished in April
1893. Forty years were employed in erecting
the building. Only members of the church
are permitted to enter it. All the public services are held at the Tabernacle, which ac-
comodates 8,000 people.

The A. M. E. Church has a flourishing congregation at this point, and manages to give
the bread of life to the church-going "Afro-
American," as they do not take kindly to the
Mormon religion. Our party spent a day and
night at this point. Visited "Saltair," the

grave of Brigham Young, and other points of interest.

Ogden a city of 15,000 population, is about twenty-five miles from Salt Lake City, and is the last city in Utah, going West. Here the tourist changes from the Denver and Rio Grande train to that of the Southern Pacific. The distance from Ogden to San Francisco is 883 miles, and the route is picturesque, historic, beautiful.

Promontory, a small place that the traveller would pass by without imagining that there was anything to be seen worthy of attention, is a place of more than ordinary historic interest. At this point, on Monday, May 10th, 1869, the Union Pacific Railroad, building West, and the Central Pacific building East, met. The news was immediately flashed all over the world that the great Trans-continental railroad of America was finished. The golden spike was driven by the late Senator Leland Stanford.

The run through Nevada has many points of interest. In the "Desert" there are many towns; and passing beyond the Valley of the Humbolt, we come to the "Lake Region," where are the Humbolt, Carson, Mud, Winnemuca, Pyramid, and Walker's Lake.

The highest point reached in the Sierra Nevadas is at Summit, where the elevation is 7,017 feet. Perhaps the most famous point is Cape Horn, which is sometimes referred to as the scenic wonder, where the train rolls around a mountain side upon a bed that was hewn there by men who were suspended from the mountain side by ropes till they cut a foot-hold.

Sacramento, the Capital of California, is our next stop. Here is a population of over 32,000 and this is a beautiful city. The African Methodist Episcopal Church is the only "colored" church there. We spent a night and day here, and the good people gave us a hearty welcome, placing at our disposal the comforts of their homes, and showing us around the city, taking in the various points of interest, including the capitol.

Passing by Oakland without stopping, we at last reached San Francisco, the spot toward which we had been looking for many days. Our first surprise was to witness that almost all the houses are frame; but this, the people say, is from fear of earthquakes. We have not heard of one in "Frisco" for a long time, but the people prefer to be on the safe side.

Since this writing the city has been visited by an earthquake.

We spent several days here, visiting Oakland frequently, which is just across the river. The city is quite hilly, and the cable-car system is in general use. Chinese are here in large numbers; they live together principally, their district—Chinatown, as it is called—embraces several blocks. Cheong Sue, our guide through Chinatown, says that a few years ago there were 80,000 Chinamen in San Francisco, but now he thinks there are not more than half that number. They are quite industrious, having stores and shops of every description, besides being engaged in the wood and coal business, and various other vocations. But they do not seem to adopt the American way of living. They hold their citizenship in China, and send their money there in large sums.

Our guide informed us that he had lived in this country for more than thirty years and seemed quite willing to end his days here, but he was not willing to cut off his "pigtail" nor dispose of his opium pipe.

Sutro Heights, just above the "Cliffs," is a point of special interest in "Frisco." Here a very wealthy gentleman, of Jewish extrac-

tion, Adolph Sutro by name, has the most
beautiful home and private park and home
that we have ever seen anywhere. Flowers of
every description, almost every imaginable
design of growing flowers, beautiful walks,
statuary, and even a managerie are here, and
the place is kept in perfect order by a number
of men who are constantly employed. In approaching the garden, one is met by a floral
design, growing on the hillside, with the following words: "Welcome to Sutro Heights."
The park is open constantly to the public, and
no tourist to San Francisco is willing to leave
until he has visited this most beautiful place.

Descending the hill from Sutro Heights, we
come to the Cliff House, where a good view
is had of the Seal Rocks, upon which are hundreds of seals, or sea loins. These animals
go out into the ocean and feed, then return
to the rocks and rest. The largest one is called Ben Butler, and he can be easily distinguished from the others on account of his enor-
mous size.

A few steps down from the Cliff house, and
we stand upon the shore of the Pacific Ocean,
and the journey is complete.

There is an A. M. E. Church in San Francisco and one in Oakland. Both are situated on

prominent streets. The congregation at San Francisco needs a new building and under the leadership of Rev. E. T. Cotman, who has just taken the charge, we may hope to soon see the good work under way.

On returning, we visited Marysville, a small city less than a hundred miles from "Frisco." Bishop B. F. Lee, was holding Conference here. Here we had an opportunity to meet the members of the California Conference, which was indeed a great pleasure. Our work is not large out there. Our people have not gone out in large numbers, and many who have gone partake largely of the gold-hunting spirit, and do not make much of church life. A resident Bishop is greatly needed, and Bishop Lee is arranging to spend much of his time there.

After spending a week most pleasantly at Marysville, our party started for home in good health, well pleased with the trip, and with a good deal less money in our pocketbooks than we had when we started out. The journey homeward was a pleasant one. A part of the company was left at Pueblo; a part at Denver, and the rest continued their journey to Omaha,

Nebraska, where with Rev. H. B. Parks and family we spent a few days most pleasantly.

Elder Parks is one of our strong young men, and is successfully managing the affairs of the church at this point. He is held in high esteem by the "Ministers Association," and is the only colored member of it.

Leaving Omaha, we stopped at Chicago only long enough to change cars, then continued our journey to the City of Brotherly Love, which we reached August 31st.

CHAPTER VIII.

My Election to the Bishopric

Four years is not really a long period of time, though under certain conditions, even four hours may seem long. With me the period between 1896 and 1900 had been a very busy one. I had again become quite interested in the work of the pastorate, preaching, raising money and doing general pastoral work. Bethel was alive and as active as a bee hive. Our first big rally had set a new record in raising money for local purposes, and it was our ambition to make some new records for the general church. Our first drive in this particular was for the support of foreign missions, and but for the friendly rivalry of Dr. W. D. Cook, at New York, I might have had an easy victory. As it was I barely led with a hundred and seventy-five dollars for the Easter offering.

No one appreciates defeat; and I having been defeated at the last General Conference, was anxious to let the Church know that I was still very much alive. Certain friends were insisting upon it that I must "make the race" again for the Bishopric.

The politician who is out for office has a way of saying: "I am in the hands of my friends," he, himself, being altogether the most intrested friend into whose hands he had fallen. But here was a case where certain friends had made my cause their own. I could name several whose names would be very familiar to many readers who took an active part in making up the necessary majority vote. I shall not call many names, lest it might seem to be making invidious distinctions between other friends who were loyal in their support. But there is one name that I may call with propriety, and without giving offense to any one. It was generally conceded that I did not have fair play at the '96 Conference. Not because I was defeated, but because the defeat was accomplished by foul means. I feel all the more free to say so, because the fact is generally known by those who were present. When several fabrications were resorted to without seeming to answer the purpose, the cry was raised by one inventive genius whom I afterward had a chance to brefriend: "he hates Southern men." And then boastingly said: "that will get them." It did. But the falsehood was so plainly apparent it could not continue to deceive. That it could have deceived at all was a mystery to me. I, myself, a Southerner by birth, as were my parents, and all my immediate family, and I think we all have our share of that quality of heart called patriotism, and say of our native state, "with all its faults, I love it still." Father and mother sleep in southern soil. My mother who spent her latter days with me in Philadelphia, requested, like Joseph, that her bones should be carried home for interment, and that request was cheerfully and religiously carried out.

And besides, the most of my travels for the eight years preceding the Conference of '96 had been in the South, where I met and made friendships with our Church leaders. Knowing them I came to admire them. Taken as a whole, a grander set of men—and women— cannot be found anywhere in the Church. I received many favors from them, and whenever an opportunity afforded, was glad to re-

ciprocate. There I met the older men who were
leading the forces. A Leak; an "honest John
Turner;" a Stringer, a Brooks; a Robinson;
a Goodloe, and Coffee; a Quarterman; Cole-
man and Moore; a Thomas and Wall; a Lof-
ton and Sherman; a Frazier; a Tyree, a
a Bryant; a Sterrett; a Mixon, just
then coming to the front; a Gardner, whose
son of his old age should be taken up by the
Church and educated; an A. M. Green, mighty
in debate; a Herbert and Johnson, and Handy; a Jimmerson and Reynolds; a Nichols and
Williams, and Chavis; a Bradwell, with Flipper just taking leadership among the younger
ones; with "Link" Gaines and "Archie" Carey
leaving the schoolroom for the regular work—
they are in evidence now. The list is a long
one, and only a few are mentioned. Besides,
a host of younger men, who have since taken
their places in the front ranks, many of whom
I had the pleasure of examining, coaching, and
otherwise assisting.

Dalton, Ga., was the first place visited by me
as a General Officer, and from there, year by
year, I went the rounds, mostly in the Southern Conferences, for there I got the largest
subscription list for the Review, the Columbia
(S. C.) Conference leading them all.

When my turn came for promotion, I felt quite secure among my newly-made friends, and "the boys." But, "while we slept, an enemy sowed tares." Never mind that now. It is simply recorded as unwritten history, which may be read with some degree of interest by those who have not a perfect knowledge of some of the things that were crowded into the last years of the last departed century, as it relates to African Methodism.

The sting of defeat, not simply for the want of votes, but so evidently by conspiracy, made me unwilling to have my friends again bring me forward, and I said as much to certain of them. But there was one friend who, understanding perfectly the causes which led to defeat, was determined to meet the foe again in 1900, and declared in very emphatic words, that my refusing to run would be a greater disappointment and humiliation to my friends, than to run, and even suffer another defeat. That was enough for me, for I so valued the friendship of Bishop W. J. Gaines, that a defeat would be less painful to me than for him to feel that I had, on account of cowardice or false pride, deserted the cause of my friends in the midst of the battle.

I stuck close to my work for three years, writing an occasional letter to the Recorders, and, a part of the time, by the request of Bishop Arnett, editing the "Christian Endeavor Visitor." At the same time keeping up a correspondence with certain friends while my honored and valuable friend, Bishop Gaines, was "sowing by all waters" and permitting no opportunity to pass which gave a chance to get in a word for "my friend Coppin." So many persons since my election have told me how Bishop Gaines explained to them why things happened as they did at Wilmington, in '96, and won them actively over to his cause.

When it became evident that I was again looming up, and that men who actually assisted in my defeat were declaring that I should be vindicated in 1900, an attempt was made to again compass my defeat by bringing out my friend, Dr. J. A. Johnson as a candidate, and thereby, not only divide my strength, but bring about confusion among my friends. But here the author of this new scheme reckoned without his host. Might just as well have asked Jonathan to betray David into the hands of Saul. The prompt reply, with a veritable Johnsonian emphasis, was: "I will not be a candidate for anything so long as Coppin is a candidate." What next? The foe must take the field and fight like a man, which was his perfect right, but, fight an honorable battle.

I resolved to make one visit, only one, to some center, and I chose the North Georgia Conference. Bishop H. M. Turner presided. I had two reasons for selecting this place. First, it was the home of Bishop Gaines, and he would be present; and secondly, I wanted to again meet, face to face, some of my old friends whom I met when I first went to the far South, and among them, the strong and intrepid Flipper, who, if he at all espoused a cause, was a host within himself. Here then would be the advantage if the North Georgia trip succeeded: if the presiding bishop became favorably impressed, with Dr. Fripper and Bishop Gaines, there would be three distinct forces in action, in a stronghold of African Methodism.

Bishop Turner gave me a hearty welcome. The men, my old time friends,—a host of them—manifested much enthusiasm. Young Fountain, a new voice lifted, said: "We boys are going to stand by you, just as we propose to stand by Dr. Flipper later on." Bishop Tur-

ner was "on the giving hand." He first asked
me to take the afternoon service. That was
not the best for me, tho, any service was
good. I wanted to get before the people in
general, and my special friends in particular.
It was Saturday afternoon, Bishop Turner called me to him, and said: "I want you to take
my appointment and preach tomorrow morning." I somehow felt that the suggestion was
from above, and at once I left the Conference,
and went to my room at the home of my
friend Bishop Gaines, and asked for grace to
enable me to fill that appointment, to the glory
of God, and the edification of the people.
What a glorious presence of the Divine Spirit!

When all was over and the service dismissed,
Dr. Flipper extended his hand with a word
of congratulation, and requested to see me
privately in the lecture room: ominous request! The tete-a-tete between us is still unwritten history. Suffice it to say the conversation proceded with frankness, and was pleasant, and "Joe Flipper" and I are still the old
friends that we were when I first visited
Georgia taking subscriptions for the Review,
preaching, lecturing and singing: "The Church
is moving on."

A few months later the General Conference

met at Columbus, Ohio. I led my delegation from the old Philadelphia Conference. There were two candidates from the same Conference, Dr. C. T. Shaffer, secretary of the Church Extension Society and myself. Such a condition sometimes insures the defeat of both aspirants. But, in this case, both were elected, together with Drs. E. Tyree: M. M. Moore, and C. S. Smith.

When the votes were counted, it was found that Drs. Tyree, Moore and Smith had the required numbers, and Dr. Shaffer and I were some votes short. There were two Shaffer brothers present and some votes just read "Shaffer" and were thrown out, they were neither for "Cornelius," nor "George" Shaffer: but, by counting the rejected ballots for C. T. Shaffer, he would have the required number. His friend, Bishop Grant, who was presiding, suggested that the thrown out ballots be counted for "Cornelius" Shaffer; but my friend, Bishop Gaines who was on guard, objected to such an unusual course of procedure, and only yielded upon the condition, that if the Conference agree that the rejected ballots be counted, the chairman would entertain a motion, that the rules be suspended, and L. J. Coppin elected by acclamation. This being

agreed to, the motion was put to count the
thrown out ballots for Dr. C. T. Shaffer. Immediately Dr. W. D. Chappelle obtained the
floor, and moved for the suspension of the
rules, and the election of L. J. Coppin by acclamation: the motion was carried unamious-
ly. But some one raised the point the next
morning that the discipline provides that such
an election should be by ballot. So, notwithstanding the vote was unanimous, it was decided, that to remove any question of legality,
the Secretary of the Conference be authorized to cast the vote of the Conference for L.
J. Coppin. This was agreed to also without
any objecting voice. So, I was elected twice,
which seemed to all quite sufficient.

The question is often discussed, what makes
one a Bishop, the election or the ordination.
I think it is quite correct to say, it requires
both performances to complete the work.
Surely no one wound be consecrated,—or ordained—to an office for which he had not been
elected. On the other hand, to neglect the induc-
tion into the office without the spiritual "set-
ting apart," would rob the whole procedure
of its sanctity, and make it unbiblical. There
may be a difference, even if only what might
be called a technical difference between ordi-

nation, and consecration. Any consecration
is an ordination, but, every ordination may
not be technically a consecration. Certain
disciples at Corinth had believed, and been
baptized, or, set apart by baptism. But when
Paul passed through he inquired as to whether
or not they had received the Holy Ghost, and
found that they had not! They had been baptized unto John's baptism, but there is a Holy
Ghost Baptism. The former is legal, the latter
spiritual. The former is by man—the election
if you will—the latter of God. The former
may or may not have divine approval; the latter is necessary even when the former is approved of God.

As for me, I was anxious about my consecration. The building of the Temple was by
divine plan and arrangement; but, when Solomon dedicated it, a cloud filled the house! God
accepted it. It was about this "acceptance"
that I was anxious. A good deal of the "human" had entered into the election; of this I
was well aware: all of which may have been
necessary. It seemed to have required prejudice, jealousy and spite, to get Joseph down
into Egypt, but God wanted him there. We
all have our choice of persons to perform certain rites, as baptism, and marriage; even bur-

rial of dead. And when it comes to being set apart to a holy office or function, all the more one might have a preference of person to perform the service. But, it is a rule with us, that our Bishops act according to seniority in ordaining Bishops. So I, like the rest, simply took my turn and was ordained by the next Bishop in order. This did not altogether satisfy the longing of my soul, tho I made myself satisfied. Perhaps it was better to be that way, for the selecting of some one, could have been construed as the rejecting of some others.

But, that Godly woman; veritable saint, Amanda Smith was on the ground. O, how I did wish that she might bow with me in prayer, and offer me to Him whom she knew so well, and who had so wonderfully answered her prayers, and blessed her work. But, how could this be brought about? So, I finally banished the thought from my mind, and went to my wife and informed her that I was now ready to go home for dinner; when to my surprise, but delight, she said: "would you object to my inviting sister Amanda Smith home to dinner with us?" We had at our boarding house a suite of rooms, for the purpose of privacy. There, in that "calm retreat," we three, away from the crowd and noise, and "congratulations:" there with God; alone with God, bowed in prayer. Amanda Smith prayed. I still feel to be under the influence of that prayer. It was indeed a prayer of consecration, and it seemed to me, "that heaven came down our souls to greet." I then felt satisfied, and especially so, because, what I desired had seemingly come by divine interposition.

For a long time I had desired to see Africa, our "Mother Land." I say Mother Land, because, the amalgamations Americana that slave conditions brought about gave us so many American fathers, that should such offsprings go to Africa, it certainly would not be going to Father Land. But be this as it may, I wanted to see Africa, the land of Ham. But it was far away. Much farther a few years ago than it now is. If one would go to Africa simply on a visit, it would prove to be rather expensive, requiring much time and money, neither of which I had at my command to spare in amounts so large. So, like many other desires that possessed me from time to time, I had about decided to abandon the hope of ever standing upon African soil.

At this Conference, five Bishops were elected a larger number than at any previous election. The object was, to extend our work to South Africa. We had for some time been on the West Coast; but now, by a visit by Bishop H. M. Turner to South Africa, the "Ethiopian" Church had been brought into the African Methodist fold. How peculiarly some things work out! Call it chance, call it providence; or, say, it just happened. Prophecy said the Christ would be born in Bethlehem: Caesar Augustus who knew nothing about the prophecy, and cared less, issued a decree, levying a tax upon his subjects which sent Joseph and Mary to Bethlehem. A comet that had been wandering, world without end, as comets will, got back into our solar system just in time to send some superstitious star gazers to Jerusalem to search prophecy to find out if it at all pointed to any thing that might be connected with what they thought a phenomenon. If they looked for the Christ, the records at Jerusalem said "Bethlehem," and to Bethlehem they went. And so, it "happened," that the "stork," the taxation; the royal decree as to time for collecting; the return of the comet; the decision of the "wise men" to go just at that time to Jerusalem, all converged to this centre. What a remarkable coincidence! But that is just the way that things do sometimes so strangely happen! Well, it so happened, that I was elected at a time that the Church was about to extend its work in Africa. This was the opportunity for me to realize my fondest dream. Five Bishops were elected, but who will go to Africa? As quick and as earnestly as Isaiah, I said: "here am I, send me." I hastened to make the request, and the Episcopal Committee was not slow to grant it. That Committee was only too glad to find one who wanted to go, and that one was only too glad of the chance. So here again was a coincidence.

I asked to be sent to South Africa. This field has both its advantages and disadvantages compared with our work on the West Coast. First, the climate is temperate compared with that of the West Coast, at Liberia and Sierra Leeone, which are under a torrid sun. But here, in South Africa is the language difficulty. True Cape Town, the headquarters of our work, has been so long under English rule, that the courts and schools are principally carried on in English; the trading the same. But even in Cape Town: "little London," we are obliged to hold Church services in the Dutch and native languages. But when you go out of Cape Town, "up the country" you are among either Dutch or native people altogether, and unless you can speak their language, you must have an interpreter.

Cape Town— the Cape of Good Hope—was settled years ago by Dutchmen, who made wives of the Hotentot women, the Hotentots being the Native people who inhabited the Cape. This Dutch, and Native union produced the "Cape Colored people," and the Hotentot tribes were crushed out or pushed back: the Dutch, and not the Native language is still spoken by these descendents of mixed blood parentage. Previous to the English occupation, was all Dutch. With the subjugation of the Dutch, it became Dutch and English. The Dutch people, dominant in numbers and in material possessions, forbade the Colored contingent to speak English. So, we have the unusual condition of Colored Dutchmen: "Coloured" as the English people spell it. Those who live right in Cape Town are obliged to be able to make themselves understood in English; but, just a very few miles outside of this City of nearly a hundred thousand population, there are Colored people who cannot speak a word of English.

Between my appointment to the 14th Episcopal District of the A. M. E. Church and the day of sailing, I filled some lecture engagements, as means of collecting some funds to assisting the work over there. Of course the subject of my lectures was: "Africa," or "South Africa," or "The Dark Continent." It is amazing, how much one can say upon a subject that he knows absolutely nothing about. But are there not books upon every imaginable subject? Yes, verily: "of making many books, there is no end" I soon collected a small library on various phases of Africa, its peoples etc. Those books contained a great deal of information, but most of them contained also many errors. This is such a large, interesting and important subject, that it is difficult for either a white or Colored writer to avoid being influenced by prejudice. The white man sees the African full of faults and deficiencies, which may be true; but certainly not all of the truth: while, the Colored man, in trying to correct the misrepresentations so apparent, may incline to the opposite extreme. In the books I read, I saw much about the Kafirs, and so, supposing that they were the principal tribes among whom I would have to work, I informed myself concerning them, and lectured about them before leaving America.

Now imagine my mortification when I found that there was no such tribe on the continent of Africa. The word originated among the Mohammedans, and meant, something like "infidel:" one outside of the faith: no reference to race at all except for the fact that it was the Native people of a certain place who were thus referred to. It finally came to be used opprobriously, just as in America the word "nigger" is used.

Just imagine my chagrin, when, in conversation with a Wesleyan—white—minister on the boat between Southampton and Cape Town I, informed him, with much confidence and zest, that I was on my way to South Africa, to labor among the "Kafirs," and he, with a sarcastic retort, replied: "there are no Kafirs to labor among." It was a "home blow." I could not reply. I had only "read" about them. From what I afterwards learned about the gentleman and his work among the Natives, I think he must have enjoyed the shot that took my breath. We were accused of "sheep stealing" for, after the advent of our Church, the Native people would leave their former Church relations with the white people, and come to us. It mattered not how vehemently we refused to receive them, and try to explain that our mission was only to such as had no Church home. One old lady at one of the places where we were being importuned to organize, said: "you may bring your Church here, or not, but I will never step my foot inside of another white man's church so long as I live." The fact was, they felt to be coming to their own, and for more reasons than is necessary for me to here name.

Some time ago I received a letter and before speaking more about things in South Africa, it may be of interest to the reader to have it appear here:

MacCameline Hall, Lower Providence, Pa.   Feb. 19, 1916.

Rt. Rev. Levi J. Coppin, D.D.:

Dear Bishop:—I've been intending to write to you for a long while my appreciation of the candor, simplicity, force and naive genuineness with which you tell the story of your travels and experiences in South Africa, while in charge of missions of your Church. In your book which Mrs. Ballentine and myself have read with great and unique pleasure, unique pleasure, I say. For it is rarely one can read a book such as yours, and rely implicity on the statement of every detail. The question so often rises: Is that so? Mustn't that be taken with a grain of salt? Isn't he prejudiced in that judgment? Isn't he showing the effect of race prejudice?

But in your book the atmosphere breathed through every line is so genuinely that of a Christian scholar and gentleman, every word carries conviction in itself.

And so, My Dear Bishop, I remain as ever your old friend and schoolmate (and I'm glad to be able to write myself so).

FRANK SCHELL BALLENTINE,

Editor—American Bible. Author—"Fundamental Facts of Life," etc., etc.

The book referred to is a previous publication, entitled: "Observations of Persons and Things in South Africa."

I cannot find words to express my joy at being privileged to go to Africa. stand upon its soil, view the land with my own eyes, and not simply with the eyes of others through the printed pages of books: breathe its air, whether healthful or poisonous, and know for myself: see and mingle with its people, from the raw native, nude, or in clout or blanket, to the highly civilized man who had passed through mission schools and English schools; a Dr. Edward W. Blyden, standing upon a platform in Philadelphia, U. S. A., with American scholarship at his feet, listening with breathless silence to his critical internation, and consecration. Any consecration is an ordination, but, every ordination may not be technically a consecration. Certain disciples at Corinth had believed, and been baptized, or, set apart by baptism. But when Paul passed through he inquired as to whether or not they had received the Holy Ghost, and found that they had not! They had been baptized unto John's baptism, but there is a Holy Ghost Baptism. The former is legal, the latter spiritual. The former is by man—the election if you will—the latter of God. The former may or may not have divine approval; the latter is necessary even when the former is approved of God.

As for me, I was anxious about my consecration. The building of the Temple was by divine plan and arrangement; but, when Solomon dedicated it, a cloud filled the house! God accepted it. It was about this "acceptance" that I was anxious. A good deal of the "human" had entered into the election; of this I was well aware: all of which may have been necessary. It seemed to have required prejudice, jealousy and spite, to get Joseph down into Egypt, but God wanted him there. We all have our choice of persons to perform certain rites, as baptism, and marriage; even bur-

thing about the business of the Conference. Upon obtaining this information I decided that we must have another interpreter, even if for that man alone. Whereupon, a young native man by the name of Sinamela, said: "You need not multiply interpreters: if you desire it, I will interpret for all of the various tongues that are here represented." The suggestion was acceded to, and Rev. S. H. Sinamela was appointed Conference Interpreter. Other native men in our work, who had up to that time never been out of Africa, could stand on their feet and hold conversation simultaneously in English, Dutch and two or more of the native dialects: such men as M. M. Mokone; Isaiah Sishuba; J. Z. Tantsi; H. R. Ngcayiya; C. M. Sebeta; Benjamin Kumalo, and many others.

Then there were many who are not of pure native blood, but of native tongue, and take the condition of the native. Some of those mixed bloods have become more or less prominent in national and tribal affairs. It may not be generally known thalt one John Dunn, frequently referred to as a Zulu chief, was an Englishman of unmixed blood. When I say unmixed, I mean, from all appearances. His children by the native women take the condition of their mothers, and are "Natives."

Adam Kok was a mulatto, though a mighty native chief. Dr. Abdurahman is a Malay, his wife an English woman. Hadje Ben Hassen is an East Indian.

Indeed, many persons, some of whom are educated and wealthy, would be representative in any civilized community, but, not being Europeans, they are, well, either Negro, or colored, or, Afro-any-thing-under-the-sun; since they are all the product of the various nationalities and race vareties that live on the big, and yet but half known continent.

Then, there are native men of pure blood; yes, I mean who come straight down from Ham, who are unmixed with Shem or Jepheth, who have grown up outside of "civilization," and never saw a "school," who have become strong leaders among their people; who have organized and held them together; who have taught them statecraft; given them some kind of religion and a very decided moral code. Bastardy and theft is seldom known among the native peoples before reached, influenced and dominated by modern civilization. Before civilization comes in and by force stops capital punishment, the father of an illegitimate child, will, upon conviction, be beheaded. As to the "nameless crime," it is nameless

and unknown among the uncivilized natives.
Missionaries, who would play upon the credulity of those from whom they hope to receive larger donations for work in "poor, benighted Africa," sometimes tell a story about
reaching fellow missionaries—women, as well
as men, remember—just in time to save them
from being eaten by cannibals—may God forgive them—but it will be of great importance
to note, that no missionary has ever said:
"We got to them just in time to save the men
from being murdered and the women from being raped." However willing a sensational and
unscrupulous missionary might be to misrep-
resent facts in order to make out a good case
for more liberal giving, not one will venture
his reputation upon such a falsehood as that
would be. And yet, have you not read in the
columns of your paper, a comment upon the
rape habit which said: "His old native—or
heathen—habit returned, being in the blood."
I say again, and without fear of successful
contradiction, that the "nameless" crime is
practically, not to say absolutely unknown by
native people who know nothing of our civilization (?) With many the first suggestion of
the possibility of a woman being forced was
when a slave-holding master forced a fellow-

slave woman. A case in point. It was in November, 1903, that I left Aliwal North—Cape Colony—for Mafeteng, Basutoland. Our pastor there had built a neat little Church, and knowing that I was to visit Basutoland, he planed to have the church dedicated during my visit. My trip and the dedication were published months ahead. There were no railroads in Basutoland—were not then—and so, it requires some time to get news through the country. No opportunity was left unimproved to advertise this church dedication; and that, too, by a "Bishop from America;" but more still, a Bishop of our race variety. Our minister there, Rev. Paul M. Shupinyaneng, is energetic and alert, and had planned to have a big crowd. He was not disappointed. When the day came they were there from far and near. Some had came as far as a three days' journey on horseback. Both men and women are expert in horseback riding out there.

Among those who came from a distance on horseback was a white girl from a far-away mission station. A pure white English young girl, daughter of the missionary at the place from which she came. She, too, was curious to see a colored Bishop. She made the journey alone, except for the company of her pony and little dog, whose feet became so sore from the long distance over the rough, rocky roads, that she had to dismount and take him up and carry him in her arms as she rode. She was at the parsonage when I arrived, and told me the story of how she came to be in Africa, and of her long journey to the dedication; how she would travel all day and stop over at night at a native village. I asked her if she were not afraid to make the journey alone. With a look of surprise, she asked, what would she be afraid of. Immediately seeing my mistake, I switched off, and suggested that she might have been exposed to wild beasts. But she said all the wild beasts had been killed and driven back from those parts long ago; a thing that I knew very well, for I had informed myself of that fact before taking the journey myself. I was glad to change the subject and begin talking about mission work. Her parents went to Africa when young. Their children were born there, and this young woman had never been out of the country. She was educated in her father's mission school, and could speak the native as well as the English language. I was glad to drop, and get away from the subject "fear," because I was quite ashamed to let her know that I came from a country where the morals of the people are such that it might not be safe for a woman, a young woman, to travel out in the open three days alone. I venture the guess, that she had never heard of a woman being outraged.

My business upon arriving at Cape Town was to have my church recognized as such, according to the laws of England, which are in force in all English colonies. Any denomination can hold religious services, and do purely religious work, but no minister can solemnize a marriage without obtaining permission from the Government. Of course, people do not want to belong to a church whose ministers cannot perform a marriage.

Rev. I. N. Fitzpatrick had preceded me to Cape Town—before my election—as a missionary sent by Bishop H. M. Turner, and had applied for Government recognition for our Church but failed to obtain it. I went, quite prepared to meet the demands of the Government so far as credentials from my church and from my government were concerned, and so I lost no time in presenting myself at the Office of the Colonial Secretary. I am sure the reader will be interested in knowing just how the English people proceed in such mat-

ters, and so, I herewith submit the correspondence that is of record at the Colonial
Office at Cape Town, South Africa.

Colonial Secretary's Office, Cape
Town, Cape of Good Hope, March
26, 1901.

The Right Rev. Bishop Coppin,

A. M. E. Church, Cape Town:

My Dear Bishop:—On the 26th of February last,
the Rev. I. N. Fitzpatrick addressed a communi-
cation to the then Prime Minister, reporting
that he had been deputed to come to South
Africa, (a) to confer with Government, (b) to
endeavor to explain the true position of the
African Methodist Episcopal Church, and (c) to
report on return to the Grand Conference of
1900.

The interview was held on the 2nd of March,
and Mr. Schreiner desired thereat, preparatory
to recognition in this Colony, that the Church
should be domiciled here, and have, on the spot,
some fully competent authority—such authority
being vouched for by the chief United States
Government official of the State he comes from,
and he noted as essential the production of
proof of educational qualifications on the part
of those "ordained or set apart" for whom recognition as "Marriage Officers" might be
sought.

Further, to quote from a letter he subsequently (3d idem)caused to be addressed to Mr. Fitzpatrick, the Prime minister stated:

It is of course well known that the African Methodist Episcopal Church of America possesses in that country a substantial organization, the ramifications of whose operations extend, you report, to Canada, the West Indian Islands, and West Africa, and Mr. Schreiner wishes you to understand that the Government does not oppose the extension to the Cape Colony of the legitimate work of that denomination.

The Government takes a broad view of the case, and concludes that as the status of the Rev. M. Dwane, who claimed to be the Bishop and ecclesiastical head in South Africa of the African Methodist Episcopal Church, has not yet been affirmed to the satisfaction of the Government, and it is understood that his connection with the African Methodist Episcopal Church in that alleged capacity has ceased, the full recognition of the African Methodist Episcopal Denomination as a Church organized and working in the Colony, within the meaning of the Marriage Order in the Council of 1838, has not been demonstrated to be yet due.

Under these circumstances and seeing that the Conference, whose avowed object is to place the disputed matter on a legal footing, is timed to assemble in two months, there appear valid reasons for deferring such recognition until the organization and working of the Church is placed upon a formal basis in the Colony, with the approval and sanction of the General Conference.

Now you have deposited with the Government the following documents, viz.:

1. Diploma of introduction (signed 7th January, 1900, by the chairman of the Bishops' Council and the Secretary) certifying that Bishop L. J. Coppin, D.D., is assigned to the Fourteenth district, and appointed to the supervision of our Church work in all of South Africa and elsewhere. It is noted, however, that in your letter of the 16th inst., you explain that 1901 was meant as the date of the year.

2. Certificate, 14th January, 1901, from Secretary of the Commonwealth of Pennsylvania, stating that the African Methodist Episcopal Church is a corporation under the laws of the State.

3. Authentication by Secretary of State of the United States of No. 2.

4. Certificate, 14th January, 1901, from Secretary of State of Ohio, that Trustees of the African Methodist Episcopal Church were incorporated on 25th June, 1900.

5. Authentication by Secretary of State of the United States of No. 4, and the Colonial Secretary feels satisfied that you have thereby the documentary requirements imposed by the Prime Minister in 1900, and he desires me to intimate to you that the African Methodist Episcopal Church (whereof you are a Bishop with

local oversight) is from the 12th of March, 1901
—the date of your interview with myself—
recognized by Goverment as a "Church" within the meaning of the Marriage Order in Council of 1838. It will be clearly understood, that
Mr. Graham has no intention of discussing
questions already disposed of by Mr. Schreiner,
and that consequently, no local ordination to
the Church effected prior to that date will be
accepted as valid for the purposes of the Marriage Order in Council.

It will be necessary from that date, that the
fact of any ordination by yourself of any person as "Minister" be notified to this office in
writing for record.

I am, my Lord Bishop, your Lordship's obedi-
ent servant.

NOEL JANISH,
Under Colonial Secretary,
for Colonial Secretary.

The reader will discover by reference to the
last paragraph in Mr. Janish's letter, that all
ordinations made previous to the 12th of
March, 1901, were null and void by this act of
recognition, and such persons though pre-
viously ordained could not be made marriage
officers either by me, or by any of my successors in office. Such persons could exercise
all other ministerial functions, or, even be re-
ordained.

We were a happy set in Cape Town and elsewhere in South Africa when this civil recognition was obtained. This, however, was only for Cape Colony, the fight for like recognition throughout South Africa continued, and was not obtained for the Transvaal, Orange River and Natal Colonies until 1910, under the administration of Bishop J. Albert Johnson.

My four years' administration in South Africa, 1900 to 1904, was busy and full of interest to myself, and I trust not altogether without profit to the native and mixed people of the place and to the A. M. E. Church. Some few incidents connected with my work in South Africa will be noticed in a subsequent chapter.

The General Conference of 1904 met in Chicago, and at its close I was assigned to the Seventh Episcopal District, consisting of South Carolina and Alabama. These are both African Methodist strongholds. Both have a Church school. In South Carolina it is Allen University, and in Alabama it is Payne University. Both schools are taking on university proportions since they were organized. In both cases large additions of land have been added to the original sites: additional buildings erected, curriculum of studies enlarged and improved, and the faculties strengthened. It just happened to have been under my administration that these additional lands for school purposes were secured both in Alabama and later in South Carolina. To secure them was quite a burden at the time but had they not been secured then, it would now be a much greater burden, if not an impossibility. A school may start on a small scale, and develop into a university, but not on an acre of ground. The A. M. E. Church had its birth in a blacksmith shop, and the denomination was connectionally organized in an unpretentious rough-cast building. but in extent, it is nearly world-wide, and has some church edifices that do credit to any city or denomination: some built from the foundation up, and others purchased from other denominations.

Our Metropolitan Church at the Capital of the Nation, planned and built by us, is said to be the largest audience room in the District of Columbia. The building is paid for. Our "Bethel," at Baltimore, purchased from the Episcopalians, at a cost of ninety thousand dollars, could not be built for two hundred thousand without the organ and furniture,

which would cost over fifty thousand more.
The main building is quite as large as the
Metropolitan at Washington, and has, in addition, a two-story chapel in the rear of the
main building and facing another street. The
building is paid for. The way the congregation of Bethel (Baltimore) came together,
under the magnetic leadership of its pastor,
himself a Marylander, and gathered more than
seventy thousand dollars in two years, and
more than doubled the membership, and won
the esteem, applause and practical co-operation of the citizens without regard to denominational affiliation, constitutes a new record in
African Methodism, and so far as we know, is
without a parallel in race enterprise, either as
it relates to church or state; i. e. religious or
secular activities.

At the close of the General Conference,
which met at Norfolk, Va., 1908, I was assigned to the Second Episcopal District, which
consisted of North Carolina, Virginia, the
District of Columbia, and Maryland. Four
years later, when the General Conference met
at Kansas City, Kansas—1912—I was returned
to the Second, and before the quadrennium
closed a vacancy occurred in the Seventh District, which consisted then of South Caro-

lina only, and I was by the request of the representatives of the district, appointed to fill the unexpired term. This made the second time that I had the privilege and pleasure of serving South Carolina, the State that has produced the largest number of African Methodist Bishops. The State that is second only to Georgia in its number of African Methodist members, and second to none in loyalty and devotion to the cause of "Manhood Christianity." The State that produced the pioneer educator of the race, and the pioneer missionary-chaplain that followed in the wake of Sherman "From Atlanta to the Sea." and organized African Methodism. It seems scarcely necessary to say that I refer to Daniel Alexander Payne and Henry MacNiel Turner: both of whom became Senior Bishops in the Church which they served so long and so faithfully.

I always had a desire to preside over the Sixth Episcopal District, partly because Georgia was the first state in the far South that I visited after entering public life, and partly on account of such a large number of personal friends. But, the path of duty cannot always be marked out ahead. Georgia has been well cared for in general superintendency, and has gone on multiplying Conferences and members in which respects it is without a peer in the family of African Methodism.

It will be seen, that for sixteen consecutive years my field of labor was entirely in the South. My first District being under the Southern Cross for four years, and the other twelve years, in Alabama, South Carolina, North Carolina, Virginia and Maryland, "My Maryland," where I first saw the light.

In looking over this territory, one will be surprised to see the number of men, produced in such a short time, who have shown superior strength in different ways. Some as students who have really developed a respectable degree of scholarship. Some as preachers who reached a mark above the average. More still as organizers, leaders of men, Church builders, founders of schools, and evangelists, by whose efforts as revivalists, thousands have been gathered into the Church, and have "continued steadfast in the Apostles doctrine." Some became well known, others, scarcely known beyond the narrow limits of the states in which they worked. But all the same, mighty men of valor. The world will never refer to them as educators, for instance; for they were not known as such, and according to the established meaning of the word, they were not. Yet, many of them have been responsible for the education of more persons than the average man who occupies the chair as teacher. They were determined to give to others, advantages which they themselves were denied. They have raised tens of thousands of dollars for the education of the youth. They have put their own children thru the schools, and many who, not having children themselves, have labored just as hard for the education of the children of others. Many of them, who, tho without education, could make most eloquent and convincing appeals for the cause.

I am reminded as I write of the late Lazarus Gardner of Alabama. He was always the popular speaker on "Educational Anniversary" in the Conferences. His English (?) was the most unique and purely original, I think, that an audience ever listened to. The charm of his fiery eloquence, and pungent thrusts that moved his audience to action, consisted principally in his violation of every known rule governing the English language. He could use some of the most "cross-legged" relative pronouns that it is possible for a combination of misplaced words to bring together. But no matter how he combined his words, he would, with a wit all his own—consciously or unconsciously—drive the truth right home, and carry his point.

Bishop Grant had a way of introducing an educated man to speak, saying he represented the present generation of schoolmen. Then he would bring out brother Gardiner as the "representative of the past," and often to the disadvantage of the first speaker. On one occasion, when the Educational meeting of the Conference in the interest of Payne University was being held, which meetings always closed with a collection for the School, he was not on the program. The Committee had seen fit to select two men of the Conference who were from the Schools, and more fitly represented the occasion. These speakers came forward, each in his turn, and vied with each other in showing what he knew about the general cause of education, and how learnedly he could give advice to the young men, and how beautifully a sentence could be clothed in most choice language. They both read papers; and each production was unduly long, especially so, in consideration of the fact that an appeal had to be made for funds, which meant the

very life of the School; and was, indeed, the
principal object of the meeting. As the speakers proceeded, the audience became tired, list-
less and sleepy. At last, around about eleven
o'clock at night, the last speaker finished. In
the mean time "brer" Gardiner had been turning and twisting like a man who was suffering
from what is popularly known as a pain-in-the
stomach. The instant moment the last word
fell from the lips of the last speaker, brother
Gardiner was on his feet, with up lifted hands,
and voice, exclaming, "Bishop!" When he saw
that he was recognized by the chair, and there
was no danger of some one else getting the
floor, he leisurely made a step or two toward
the presiding officer, and combining a pathet-
ic look with a cunning twinkle in his eye, which
secured the attention and interest of the house,
he, pleadingly said: "May I speak a word for
Payne?" The Bishop who fully took in the
situation, and was himself showing much anx-
iety, leaned forward, and with a humorous and
characteristic smile, said: "you may; for I think
it is about time that such a word was said."
That word was spoken. The other speakers
were forgotten, and a large contribution was
laid on the table for "Payne;" thanks to the

old hero, who had many a time saved the day when the cause seemed about lost.

Rev. R. H. W. Leak tells a story about himself. When freedom was declared, the men of thought and ambition, veritable leaders among their unfortunate fellows enslaved like themselves, gathered the people together for various purposes. The subjects they considered and the volume of business transacted soon made it necessary to have a secretary to note down their doings, and keep them straight upon what was transacted in previous meetings. Well, as Mr. Leak had been making himself very conspicuous in the meetings, some one moved that he be elected secretary. He could neither read nor write. But not willing to lose his place as one of the leaders, he would not decline the position. So, he sat down at the table where stationary was provided, and with pencil in hand appeared to be very busy. He was indeed very busy listening, exercising, and taxing his phenomenal memory, and planning to "get by." At the close of the meeting, some one called for the reading of the minutes before the final adjournment. Mr. Leak suspicioned that it was some one trying to catch him. But he was not to be trapped so easily. He rose up, faced the audience, and held up before him the paper that was supposed to contain the minutes, and drawing upon his power of memory, and exhibiting a courage and audacity as remarkable as his memory, he read (?) the minutes. When the meeting convened again, the minutes were written out, and Mr. Leak held his position as secretary. During the whole of his active life, he was the leader among the ministers of his State, and once served, by an election at the General Conference, as Manager of the Book Concern.

It was during my second term on the Second District that St. Peters Church on Druid Hill Ave., and Lanvale St., Baltimore, was purchased as the new home for Bethel. The Bishop of the District, L. J. Coppin; the resident Bishop, John Hurst; and the pastor of the Church, D. G. Hill, went on the judgment note for fifteen thousand dollars, to obtain the necessary money to bind the bargain. The old Town Bank, of East Baltimore made the loan.

The Baltimore Conference as an Incorporated body, purchased several Church sites, an Old Peoples' Home and a Cemetery. In such unselfish public work, I think the Baltimore Conference leads the Denomination. Under the leadership of Bishop J. Albert Johnson,

my successor, an effort is being put forth to
pay off the Conference indebtedness. With
such men as constitute the ministry of the
Conference to lead off in the work; with African Methodists of the original type to follow,
and, with the fact that the Baltimore Conference is, in fact, the State of Maryland, what
may we not expect?

The Centennial General Conference, 1916,
met in Philadelphia: the only proper place for
it to meet. At the close of that Conference
I was assigned to the 4th Episcopal District,
which embraces, Kentucky, Indiana, Illinois,
Wisconsin, Iowa, Minnesota, North Dakota,
South Dakota and Winnipeg Dominion of
Canada. This is the first time in twenty years
that the whole of my District has not been
on Southern soil.

The centre of the work, and the centre of
attraction is Chicago:—on the Lake:—the
City of the West. But the whole of the District is most interesting. The blue grass of
Kentucky and its fine horses have advertised
the State to the world. Whiskey also came
in for a share of notoriety, but just now, the
bar rooms are closed: let us hope forever. But
the noble men and women are still there; and

the blue grass, and the fine stock, and the climate.

The A. M. E. Chuch undertook years ago to maintain a school there; but the State gave better school facilities than we could: and besides, Wilberforce is so near, so that those who wished the addition of religious training could go there. Consequently "Wayman Institute" was finally closed.

More than twenty-five years ago I visited Kentucky—"Old Kentucky"—for the first time. I was editor of the A. M. E. Review. Bishop A. W. Wayman was holding a Conference at Covington. On account of the smallness of our Church there, the sessions were held in the Church of a sister denomination. While I appreciated highly the kindly feeling, and spirit of brotherhood that apparently existed there, I thought, that if we needed a Church Society there, we needed a building large enough to do all of our Church work in. One of the reasons I had for aspiring to the Bishoprick, was, that I might have a broader field of opportunity, to accomplish some things that I considered were much needed. We are now building a representative Church at Covington. Have just finished a splendid one at Harrodsburg, and bought another one at Louisville. In other portions of the State, also, new Churches have been built, or are in course of erection.

I once visited Richmond, Va., the old Confederate Capital, and found that our Church there that was once number one, occupying a rather insignificant place among the large and influential churches there. I decided that if I ever got a chance, I would certainly endeavor to bring "Old Third St." back to her former and proper place. The opportunity came, and it is now in Class A.

Our work in the 4th District, embraces the city where sleeps the dust of William Paul Quinn, the pioneer Bishop of the West, who was buried at Richmond, Indiana. At our last Presiding Elders' Council, arrangements were made to properly mark his grave. He is buried in one of the public cemeteries, at a prominent place along a main drive; and since Richmond has been sufficiently civilized to make no discrimination as to his resting place, it seems but our bounden duty to place at the grave a stone that will be in keeping with the prevailing monuments there.

The "World War" opened the way for a general migration of our people from the

South to the East, West, and Northwest,
Chicago being a great industrial centre, many
thousands were induced to come there, even
to the extent of creating a housing problem,
with all else that would naturally follow such
a sudden influx of population, and that in such
large numbers. Not the least among the
things necessary to meet such a condition was
sufficient churches, and Christian workers, to
prevent the moral degradation that would be
sure to follow, if nothing in particular was
done to prevent it. Our Church was put to
the test like other Churches. We needed social workers in the different ramifications of
Sociology, which, while it was not at all foreign to routine church work, meant special
workers, more workers, larger means, larger
church buildings and more of them. It also
meant that in the civic activities of so large
a city, the race had need to find some person
or persons, who could take the initiative in
looking after the interests of our people especially. The Hebrews, and other race varieties looked after their people; why not we?
It is a fact worthy of note, and historical preservation, that in the person of Dr. A. J. Carey
one of the ministers in Chicago, the A. M. E.
Church furnished the only Colored man to sit

as Chairman of a Board of Exemption, any
where in the United States. Thousands of
white and colored men alike had to pass his
Committee. Illinois in general, and Chicago
in particular raised their quota of men and
money for the greatest conflict of human history: and there we were, with a representative strong and aggressive, to see to it that
a "square deal," equal opportunity, encouragement and credit were given to one of the most
loyal units that make up America's Cosmopoli-
tan Citizenship. Fortunately, our pulpits of
Chicago and vicinity were ably filled at this
most important period of our history, and the
Churches were intelligently directed in their
legitimate work of caring for the soul without
neglecting the body. Our women led their
forces, gathering larger amounts than ever before for purely mission work. The Y. W. C.
A. work, with one of our own girls, Miss Edna
Cook as the Secretary, took on new life, and
was among the active agencies for directing
young womanhood. Our Stewardesses and
Deaconesses, many in number, were alert and
aggressive in their work, and rendered invaluable service. The fact is, the whole machinery of the Church was operated vigorous-

ly, and every department seemed to catch the spirit of the times.

A recent report from the Chicago Churches, thru the Presiding Elder, covering the period of active immigration, shows that five thousand, two hundred and sixty-four accessions were made to the Chicago Churches alone. Two new churches built, two bought, and five new Societies organized. At the time this report was handed in a movement was under way to purchase two more Churches. These figures show to an extent, the activities of our Denomination in meeting the wants of the new comers. With this, plus all the activities of the other Denominations, notably the Baptist and Methodist Episcopal, there was still a large contingent to be caught by the world forces; and especially so because of the "open door" privileges, compared to the ostracism of the Southern sections of the country, from which the influx of people came.

The close of the present quadrennium, May, 1920, will mark the forty-third mile stone of my ministerial career, and the twentieth in the Bishopric. In these pages of "Unwritten History," the story of my life has been told in a measure, and worthy deeds of many others, otherwise unknown to posterity, have been narrated. The reader may have at least the interest that can be had in reading a novel, with the additional interest that may be produced by fact, versus fiction. There is nothing startling, to start a youth off on a "Red Rappo" dash, to acheive fame, commit murder, discover a new world, or turn the old one up side down. But in the simple narration of ordinary things about ordinary people, there may be found some hints that may be suggestive to some one who is earnestly seeking to know what after all is really worth while in life. Kingdoms, and thrones are tottering, and falling. The head that wears the crown is more "uneasy" than ever. The old word Democracy is having a new interpretation, even if more just now in theory than in practice: but righteousness, justice, sincerity, the Golden Rule, "naked" TRUTH, unchanged in meaning or purpose; undaunted in their DETERMINATION to take their rightful place in human affairs, lift their voice, and ever cry; "be not deceived, God is not mocked."

CHAPTER IX

Domestic Bliss: With Shadow and Sunshine.

I loved a maiden, fair and pure,
And could no ill foresee.
She was the idol of my heart,
And all the world to me.

And she, in love and confidence,
Laid bare her heart, so true.
Thus panoplied with love, we thought
We could the world subdue.

Alas! poor simple-hearted pair,
With calculations large,
We hastened down to life's big sea
And launched our little barge.

The day was bright, the sea was calm,
The wind and tide were fair.
We hoisted sails and onward sped,
A joyous happy pair.

But soon a dreadful storm arose
Upon the treacherous sea.
And then we cried: "O cruel fate,
Canst thou so heartless be?"

(345)

With two we started on the voyage,
With three the storm came on:
But when the darkness disappeared
Behold there was but one.

Here is the story briefly told: I wooed and won Miss Martha Grinnage, a school teacher of Wilmington, Del. Our marriage took place in September 1875. The marriage ceremony was performed by the Rev. John F. Thomas, by whom I was afterwards licensed to preach.

The stork seemed so impatiently solicitious for our further happiness that he came on scheduled time with our boy "Octavius Valentine."

Octavius Valentine Cato, professor at the "Institute for Colored Youth," was murdered at the election polls about this time, and was everywhere referred to as hero and martyr. This accounts for the name of our first born son, who might have otherwise been "junior." Nine months after the birth of our boy, he was taken from us by the cold, ruthless hand of death; and just eighteen days later his mother followed. Thus, in the brief period of eighteen months, my first matrimonial experience was brought to a close. Blessed Mother! A sweet spirit: bright of intellect:

away beyond her years in wisdom, prudence, and all that goes to constitute noble woman- hood. Patient in affliction, strong in faith, she accepted her lot; gave up her babe with the resignation of a Christian heroine, and with- out a murmur surrendered her own life to Him who gave it.

Mother and Child! "Earth is too rude for thee; Heaven will be glad of thee; Come away lovely ones, come to thy rest."

But, as for me! I left Wilmington as quickly as possible; away from the scenes that recalled a sadness, that overshadowed all the preceed- ing joys that the place could recall.

I was young and strong, of body, and tried with all my heart to say: "Thy will be done," and to seek more diligently than ever to know His will concerning me. I cannot describe the blow, and will not try. I seemed stunned. I am glad that I had faith in God, and felt that I could leave it all to Him. I did not seek any other source of comfort, nor look elsewhere for direction as to my future. I was teaching school at the time, and had but a short time before this terrible ordeal been licensed to preach.

With this new experience, I began to think less of the school house, and more and more about the ministry. Every voice seemed to call this way; every circumstance seemed to point in this direction; and the following spring, by the leading of the divine Spirit, and the advice of my pastor Rev. John F. Thomas, and Dr. B. T. Tanner, I joined the Philadelphia Conference "on probation," and began as stated elsewhere, my ministerial career as City Missionary in Philadelphia. This was the spring of 1877.

Up to this time I had not received any special training in theology. I say special training, meaning, that which takes up the subject scientifically, with a priori, and a posteriori evidence:—of things not seen—with homiletical and hermaneutical arrangement, and discussion in sermonizing. I had been a student of the Bible—had read it from "lid to lid" I once heard two old Methodist ladies talking upon the subject of religion, preaching, etc. One asked the other what Doctor of Divinity meant. The reply was: "it means Master of the Bible." How I wished that I was a doctor of divinity! And I never changed my mind until I became personally acquainted with a few of them. Mr. Moody was not a D. D.,he would not even permit you to call him Reverend. Rev. Henry Ward

Beecher was a D. D., but every body just said:
"Henry Ward Beecher." The same thing was
true of Philips Brooks. Those names stood
for more than any qualifying letters or titles
that could be attached to them. The "Shu-
nemite" called Elisha: "Holy Man of God."
But he was a school man: I mean, he was a
theological school man, as was Henry Ward
Beecher, and Phillips Brooks. The schools
systemitize the work, and teach the student
how to find out the things that he wants to
know. Many a man, "a diamond in the rough;
has gone thru the schools, and come out a
"polished shaft."

So soon as I entered the ministry, I took
up the "Course of Studies" laid down in the
Discipline; and Latin and Greek besides—Hebrew and German later on—preparatory to a
regular theological course which is spoken of
in another chapter.

I was hailed as a "single young minister;"
and in Philadelphia. Both in my Mission and
elsewhere, there were a plenty of young girls
of marriageable age who might, upon a proper
presentation of the subject, have been induced
"to enter the ministry." But, besides a lingering memory of one who, though "at rest," was

entitled still to due respect, was a burning desire to "make full proof" of the ministry.

My pastoral work was not very taxing, and that gave much time for study. This was especially true of the first two years, while at the Mission. Four years by due course, brought one up to full fledged ministry. The first two, as Licentiate, on probation: the next two, as Deacon, full member of Conference, but not in full orders. At the end of the fourth year, if the student regularly passed the classes, he was entitled to his ordination to the Eldership. I made my four years course in three years, but, by an understanding which I had with myself upon entering the ministry, I refrained from keeping company with ladies during the full four years of the usual probationary period. I did not see how I could give much attention to a subject so important and absorbing as that of: "Love, Courtship and Marriage," and yet make the progress in my ministerial work and studies that I had planned.

Toward the close of the fourth year, A Fair was in progress at the Masonic Temple on 11th St. It was being held in the interest of the Christian Recorder, the oldest Negro journal in America: perhaps in the world. Miss

Fanny M. Jackson, Principal of the Institute for Colored Youth," was the prime mover, and President of the Fair Committee. Miss Jackson was a member of the Episcopal Denomination, but was known to be public spirited: and seeing that the Recorder was hindered in its usefulness by being burdened with debt, Miss Jackson got together a number of friends of various denominations, and resolved to raise some money for the "Book Concern" and Recorder.

A correspondence was kept up thru the Recorder columns for some months. Contributions of articles of any kind suitable for a Fair were solicited. More than a thousand dollars were cleared by the effort, and handed over to the Manager, Dr. H. M. Turner. Speaking from memory, I believe the amount was about seventeen hundred.

This Fair brought the people of the different denominations together as never before. Philadelphia—whether to its credit or not—had the reputation of being cold, stiff, conservative. Many who were born in Phila., belonged to the "Quaker City Society," an organization that only those of Phila. birth could join. Some who, tho thus qualified, would not join, because this would put them into close social relations with some whom they would not ordinarily associate with. As to the Church people, while there was not any visible, or, open denominational hostility, the most part found enough to engage them at their own Churches.

African Methodists easily led in the number of members. Here the independent movement by Richard Allen, began and the sect multiplied. Bethel was the "old fireplace." Thither the crowds went! Then Union, and Campbell Chapel, and Mount Pisgah, and Zion were lusty daughters, with "Little Wesley" and a number of smaller bodies were of promise. St. Thomas was the mother Episcopal Church, with Crucifixion a mission, where Miss Jackson held membership and sang on the choir: an attractive alto voice.

Miss Jackson, a graduate from Oberlin College, with "gentleman's course," had made an innovation by becoming the Principal in a High School, that graduated its pupils in Greek, Latin and Higher Mathematics. Octavious Cato, a teacher in the sceintific department informed the Managers of the Institute that he would not teach under a woman. The Managers declined to consider his objection, and he, like many a wise man, changed his mind.

Miss Jackson was not only the recognized scholar among school teachers, but gained a reputation of being a platform speaker with few equals even among the other race varieties. These facts, backed up by an irreproachable character, gave her undisputed leadership in all matters of race advancement. She was the one person whom the whole city would follow, even to the extent of forming an Undenominational Committee, for helping a denominational enterprise.

The Fair had a popular following, and became quite a social centre during the month of its existence.

This was my fourth year in the city, and, as fully explained in another chapter, I was pastor at the Mother Church: as such, I felt that whatever influence I had, and could bring to bear upon my Church, should be used to make the Fair a success.

I attended the fair night after night, and every night: partly because it was in the interest of our own Concern, and partly because it had become a very pleasant place for people, especially young people to gather.

Miss Jackson, a hard and constant worker for the public good, was not a society woman. She was conspicuously absent from the dance, public and private, and from such delicate little social features, as the "card parties" and like evidences of social standing that the elite of society people hold dear. She was just as conspicuous for her presence, however, at all public gatherings for social and moral uplift.

For reasons, evidently satisfactory to herself, she declined the company of gentlemen, and was known to go and come anywhere, and everywhere alone.

But here is a case, where she will be out after midnight, night after night for a month, and that, in a portion of the City where a certain class of men and women could be seen on the street at any late hour of the night, or early hours of morning, and they would not be attending prayer meeting either, nor going to "the Fair."

To meet this new condition Miss Jackson engaged the janitor of her school to see her safely home from the Fair every night: to be more exact, every morning. This was no part of his duty as janitor, and he got extra pay for it. My friend John S. Durham seemed to know all about it, and explained the matter fully to me. When I put the question squarely to him, as to why Miss Jackson went to such trouble and expense, he replied saying, that it was because she did not accept the company of gentlemen in a social way.

After we had discussed the matter a bit, I ventured the suggestion, on a wager from my friend, that before that Fair closed, I would have "John Williams"—the janitor—dismissed, and take his place.

I had a sort of fondness for daring, any way. When I was a boy, if I wanted to throw "Aunt" Jemima—Aunt Mimy—into a nervous fit, I would climb up the big tree in the yard, and stand on my head on a limb. Or mount an unbroken colt without a bridle, and let him see how fast he could run. Or fight a boy twice my size. David, of all Bible characters, was my hero. In school, I always considered that my place was at the head of the class. In the ministry, had I not reached the Mother Church in two years? Sure enough, I went there by accident, but, how did I stay there? I am free to confess, that I was shy of Miss Jackson; but it was not a matter of life and death. A little mortification was about the worse thing likely to happen.

I made the venture and succeeded. Mr. Williams once displaced, never got his job again. Before the Fair closed, I was seeing Miss Jackson home every night: and more, was having business with her during some of the days: business pertaining to the Fair, of course! But, all the same, business that made it necessary for me to call at the Institute about the closing hour. The fact is, I became interested in Miss Jackson, and she became interested in me. She had a fixed course in life, and stubbornly maintained it, until it became a fixed habit. I dared to encounter her. Perhaps she admired my courage. I found much in her to admire. Our coming together was like the dropping of seed into the earth, which grew.

Miss Jackson had a heart with a deep well. How to reach it was the only question. It did not appear upon the surface. Dazzling intellect is what was seen and constantly spoken of. But there was a heart, which, if once reached, would pour out its love like a perennial spring. Her intellect was great, but her heart was greater.

We were married December 21st, 1887, by Bishop D. A. Papne, assisted by Rev. Henry L. Phillips, in the 19th St. Baptist Church, Washington, D. C. My Bishop, her pastor and her sister's Church. "At Home" 51 Centre St., Baltimore, Md. At that time I was pastor of Bethel Church, Baltimore, as the reader will recall. It was but a nine days wonder, and the people ceased to speak of the strange thing that had happened: all, however, but one crazy girl, named Carry Robinson, who entered a suit against me for a breach of promise. Her first lawyer died before the case was called, as did also the second. The third one employed tried the case, and lost. "Last of all, the woman died" It is supposed to have been a case of black mail: likely inspired by some one who did not appear on the scene. Lawyer number three offered to compromise the case out of Court for three hundred dollars. But I was obdurate. The plan was to affect a compromise before the case was called, and give me a chance to avoid "embarrassing my bride." But, as I was innocent, and my bride had confidence in me, I concluded that the best thing to do, was to clean up the matter root and branch.

During this marriage, I was pastor, and editor of the Review, and wife remained in the school room. There are two ways to stop an automobile, viz, to slow down, or, to run the machine against a stone wall, or a tree. I desired that my wife should give up teaching at once, but the school room habit clung, and it seemed wiser to eliminate it gradually. The A. M. E. Church had organized its women into a "Mite Missionary Society," the chief object of which was to foster foreign Missions. The Churches organized at will, held meetings monthly or quarterly, according to the inclination or activity of those at the head of the Society. Many of the Churches had no Missionary organization at all. The money collected was used for the work in Haiti, and West Africa. It was paid out by the officers of the Mite Society that raised it, thru the direction of the Home and Foreign Society, with office at New York. It was indeed a good and useful work that the women of the Church were engaged in, but the amount of money that was being raised was inadequate to the needs, and was much less than the Church properly organized was capable of raising. Mrs. Coppin saw what was needed to put new life into the societies already in existence and also to create others.

When the General Conference met in Philadelphia, in 1892, Mrs. Coppin appeared at one of the sessions with a constitution, which, if

adopted, and put into common use, was destined to revolutionize the Mite work, by having each Conference, a Conference Branch,
and at each Charge, an auxiliary Society, whose
officers should constitute the Conference
Branch, and that more attention should be
given to the Home work. The General Conference adopted the Constitution, and the work
sure enough took on new life, so that, a single
Conference now actually raises more for Mis
sion work than the whole Church—thru the
women—raised previous to 1892.

One of the reasons given by Mrs. Coppin
for not wanting to give up teaching at once,
was, that she had begun a campaign in the
interest of Industrial Education. Her contention was, that the only way for a Philadelphia boy—Colored—to get a trade, was to
commit an offense for which he would be put
into the House of Correction. Even then, the
trades were few and all of a kind, such as
making brooms, and caning chairs. None of
the various industries of Philadelphia a veritable industrial center, would take a colored
apprentice. This campaign was continued
with public speeches in Philadelphia and vicinity; in Churches, and other places of public
assembly, until it became a real propaganda.

Every body was pleading for Industrial as well as Literary education for the youth.

The Managers of the Institute for Colored Youth at last became interested to the extent that the Institute grounds were enlarged, extending from Bainbridge St., thru to South, and buildings were erected in which were taught carpentry, brick masonry; plumbing; plastering; shoe making; dress making; tailoring; needle work and cooking. Inside of the large building, a house would be erected, with all the modern improvements, then, torn down. From the Institute went classes of boys, during vacation, and built rows of houses. There were night classes for those who were beyond school age. Men who were carrying the hod learned to be stone masons. Some from those night classes learned carpentry and became contractors.

I think it is not generally known that Industrial Education for Colored Youth had its origin in Philadelphia and not at Tuskegee. It is none the better for that, but, it is a historical fact, and, perhaps, unwritten.

Another thing that Mrs. Coppin was always anxious about, was a proper place for girls to live, who came from other States—and from outside of the City—to study at the Institute.

She desired to have some kind of home that might be under the supervision of the Institute management. Our own home was opened for girls from South Carolina, North Carolina, Georgia and Virginia. The number so increased, that a ten room dwelling next door was rented as a girls' dormitory, and between that, and a portion of our own home, we had as many as fifteen girls at one time. Some of them paid board—that was before war prices —others were given a chance to do light house keeping at the dormitory. We paid the rent.

We tried to follow up our dormitory girls to see what they made of their lives. To my personal knowledge some married College Professors; some ministers; some remained single and taught. I think they all did well. They went out into the world with a feeling that, on account of the influences by which they had been surrounded, and the care bestowed upon them, they must give a good account of themselves. They became more or less imbued with the ways and ideals of "Miss Fanny"—the name by which they still refer to her—.Of the hundreds of young women who gaduated from the "Institute," I do not know of one who is not to some extent influenced by the peculiar moral and ethical training re-

ceived there. The Institute was not a City
school under Management of the Board of
Education, and for that reason the graduates
could not teach in Philadelphia, without the
City's certificate; but, in New Jersey, Delaware and Maryland, Institute Graduates could
teach without further examination. The fact
is, the Institute carried a higher curriculum
than the City High Schools.

With the Industrial regime fully established,
Mrs. Coppin began to "slow down" preparatory to giving up teaching. My election to
the Bishopric and assignment to South Africa
gave the opportunity to gracefully withdraw
from a work that had really become second
nature.. I organized "Bethel Institute" at
Cape Town; Mrs. Coppin did not teach there,
but devoted her energies in organizing Mite
Societies, and training the "Native" 'and
"Colored" women for Christian work. She
went with me into the interior as far as thir-
teen hundred and sixty miles from Cape
Town; to the country of the late warrior
chief, Lobengula; into Rhodesia as far as
Bulawayo.

The natives and colored women of Africa
were delighted to have one of their sisters
from America to come over and be with them

in the formative period of their church work. Africa is not unlike other portions of the world in its habit of holding the women back. The coming of Christianity everywhere marks the beginning of woman's emancipation. Christianity in Africa must not mean less.

It is a fact that one has pleasure in noting with especial emphasis, that our African women, though just emerging from the slavery that is naturally entailed by the custom of polygamy, are really enthusiastic Christian workers. They so soon learn that Christianity is not simply something to believe or recite, but, something to be, and to do.

Bishop Johnson tells a story about his saying to the women of one of his South African Conferences, that he wanted them to raise a certain amount of money for missionary purposes; that is, to open new missions. They answered that they would let him know the next day, whether they thought they could raise it or not. So, they had a season of prayer and continued in the meeting all night.

They wanted that one of the buildings at the Wilberforce Institute should be a memorial; and so, they called it: The Fanny Jackson Coppin Hall. For this building ten thousand dollars were raised right there on the mission field.

I returned from Africa in the Spring of 1904, and was assigned to the Seventh District, embracing South Carolina and Alabama. Mrs. Coppin was then in declining health, and could not accompany me through the whole of the district, but did go through portions of South Carolina.

Years of constant and strenuous work began to tell on an iron constitution that had responded so faithfully to the call of duty. For eight years, that unique personality, so accustomed to be before the public in every racial and civic discussion, was practically confined to the house. This confinement was not caused by any organic troubles, nor anything bordering on a lingering illness, but a gradual breaking down of the constitution. A lack of strength to engage in anything that drew heavily upon the physical energies. The mind was the last to succumb. It was, indeed, a great blessing and source of happiness that during this long period of enforced retirement from physical activities, the mind should retain its strength and vigor, so that the daily papers, magazines and books, especially the Bible, still held their charm; and also the keenest interest was had in conversing upon current topics.

A treatise entitled: "Reminiscences of School Life, and Hints on Teaching" was produced during this quiet period. It is not a pretentious, labored production: the story "reminiscences" is told in the simplest possible way, and the "hints" are of the most primary and practical kind. Any one who knew the author well can see traces of that simplicity that characterized her life. Herself a classical scholar of acknowledged ability, preferred always to teach primary branches, with the explanation that this was the formative period of life and too much attention could not be given to fundamental work.

This service closed a life of unusual activity, of a most unselfish nature. One of the many eulogies following her demise, sums up thus: "For forty years she was the inspiration of thousands. Her name was a synonym for character, for high inspiration, for purity, for thoroughness and for righteousness."

The end came January 21st, 1913. The shadow again lowered over my home, after a longer period of sunshine. This time, with more life behind me than before me, making a decision as to how to spend the remaining years that might follow, far more difficult than when the first shadows passed.

Had my friend Bishop John Albert Johnson been near at this sad moment I would not have felt quite so much alone. Friends indeed were near; and relatives, with abundant sympathy to pour out without stint.

In this hour of loneliness and sadness representatives of the Second District over which I presided came in numbers. From North Carolina, and Virginia, and Maryland, and from the District of Columbia they came to our home in Philadelphia. Telegrams and letters numerous came.

At the funeral at Bethel Church, Dr. Henry L. Phillips, friend and ex-pastor, suggested a suitable monument, and one that of all things the deceased would like, wouid be a scholarship for struggling youth, seeking an education. Following this suggestion a few friends were called together for consultation, and a "Fanny Jackson Coppin Scholarship" was instituted, and afterwards incorporated under the laws of the State of Pennsylvania, and the Provident Life and Trust Company of Philadelphia, made the fiscal agent, to hold and invest the funds, the interest of which alone goes to sustain scholarships.

The movement was inaugurated by a gift of one thousand dollars, which was followed by smaller amount. The thought was to get a few thousand in hand and invested before giving out a scholarship; and by continuing to add to the principal, the interest would in time become sufficient to sustain several scholarships at a time.

Donations and bequests can be made at any time, and it is to be hoped that the Fund will grow into many thousands.

For a time I seemed to be up into the air. This seems like a strange way to express it, but what I mean is so difficult to express. We had learned to live within each other. This was especially true of the last eight or ten years. Before this, both lives were so busy that each could easily become absorbed in the duty at hand. At the last, my "duty," and privilege and pleasure, was to live alone for her who had lived for so many; and she, now, unable to live the old life that was as broad as humanity itself, could only live for and depend upon one.

I comforted myself by deciding that however imperfectly lived, my life had amounted to something. I had written a book on "The Relation of Baptized Children to the Church," my pet subject from early life; and one on "The Key to Scriptural Interpretation," the subject that I had thought most about during my ministerial life. I had been to Africa, and realized my life's dream, and had even written on "Observations of Men and Things in South Africa." Why not stop right here? But as comforting (?) as were those considerations, they did not comfort. So, not knowing what to do, I decided to do nothing. Just live a "come day, go day" life. Do no harm, and not be over anxious about doing any more good. But this did not satisfy. Everything about my life seemed so indefinite, uncertain, unreal, "up in the air" like. That which came nearest being real was a cigar. I "took to smoke." Thank God I did not take to drink. I smoked by day, and by night, and got up out of the bed and smoked. This began to tell on my bodily strength. I would be tired instead of being refreshed when morning came. I did not enjoy reading, and only did such work as I was obliged to do, and that just in a sort of perfunctory manner.

A friend remarked that I needed companionship at home. He meant well, but had I spoken the first words that came to my mind I believe he would not have thought well of

me. I felt stung at the remark. I was standing only a year from an open grave.

But I am more and more convinced that
Providence has much more to do with human
affairs than we are wont to acknowledge.
How suddenly, and, it would seem, mysteriously a change in my course and in my feelings came!

I chanced to meet Dr. M. E. Thompson, a
practicing physician in Baltimore, Md. I
thought it so strange, that after a brief conversation with her, and that, too, upon the
subject of her professional work, I should be
unable to dismiss her from my mind after we
parted. If I should decide that the impression was only momentary, such a decision
would be proved false, by the fact that the impression continued. Should I decide that it
was due to the interest I had in the subject
of our conversation, that, too, would be over-
ruled by the fact that I really thought nothing more about the subject. An image fixed
itself in my mental vision, and in my thought.
An image that I could see with closed eyes.
A voice that I could still hear, though inau-
dible. A thought, evesdropping ever and anon,
no matter what other thoughts might engage
the mind. It would seem indeed that there

was but one course to decide upon in such a
case, and that to harken to the persistent voice.
To return to the object of the lingering
thought, and try to discover the cause of its
obstinacy. This I could not get the consent
of my own, real mind, to do. My own purpose and thought seemed quite different from
this interloping thought, that came of itself,
and was neither asking permission to stay,
nor direction as to its course.

But, I, too, was persistent. Had I not years
and experience at my command? Such a
strong feeling in early manhood would have
met no opposition, but it is different now.
And so it was, that age and experience instituted a pitched battle with a strange and
unfamiliar impression, and I decided to let
them fight it out.

We hear much about "love at first sight."
This, I think has been the experience of many.
But, in such a case, I take it, that all the
mental powers are in accord with the impression: that reason and judgment are dethroned, and desire makes common cause with the
emotion, and no discordant note is heard. In
the first place the object of the impression is
not repugnant to such a visitation, and makes
no fight against it. In the leading of Provi-

dence, however, some things may happen, that
seem entirely outside of the ordinary course
of events: a sort of wheel within a wheel:
something added to the ordinary, and this
seemed to be the case with me. Reason and
judgment were not dethroned. Indeed, they
never seemed more active in the legitimate
exercise of their functions, nor more unable
to fully control the situation. Accustomed to
arbitrary action in all cases, they now agree
to arbitrate whatever the newcomer refuses
to sanction.

I met Dr. Thompson again. Engaged her in
conversation, venturing a little beyond medical
subjects, but not daring to disclose the fact
that there was a soul struggle raging within,
and that she was the unconscious cause. This
meeting was at an Annual Conference that I
was holding at one of the Baltimore churches.
The doctor was among the visitors who were
introduced to the Conference, and asked to
speak. The ease, cleverness, and evident sincerity with which she spoke, certainly did
not contribute anything toward banishing
that anxious thought of her that had been
gripping me so irresistibly since the first
meeting. The address was so free from that
sophomoric air, and tone that so often char-

acterizes the speech of professional people before popular audiences. Men are even now so inclined to either discount the ability of the woman physician, or to regard her as, at least, being on trial, that it would not have been a great wonder had this young woman felt called upon to utilize this opportunity to prove that her certificate was held by merit.

The Conference was a religious meeting. The business was, reports from Christian workers. The prevailing thought, necessarily was, the performance of duty; how performed; the great harvest field, and the call to all for service. The doctor readily caught the spirit of the meeting, and with perfect ease addressed the body.

When we separated this time I was ready to decide that the persistent impression was victorious. But the end of the first struggle could only mean the beginning of another. Up to this time it had only been "my heart and me;" but now, if the matter proceeds any farther, another "me" and another "heart" must be apprised and consulted.

This required both courage and tact. It required more courage than I felt to be immediately in possession of. I must wait for a propitious moment. Would it come? Had not two fairly favorable opportunities, at least for an introduction of the main subject been allowed to pass unimproved? Will all things come to him who has patience to wait? Well, that depends. Patience may accomplish many things, but certainly not "all things."

I may be regarded by some as either superstitious, or presumptious, but from an early period of my life I have entertained the idea that Providence had much to do with directing my course. The idea may have first originated from what my mother had to say about the "Christmas baby": but besides that, I have observed certain events in my life that I could not satisfactorily account for without admitting of providential interposition. So, I concluded that if Providence had anything at all to do with this business in hand, a door of opportunity would in some way be opened; and it was.

Now, I am sure, the curiously inclined would not object to knowing all about the succeeding steps leading up to the final conclusion, but this would not be of any especial historic value.

The Conference referred to was held in April: the three months following were full of interest to me, and the course that events took got the doctor seriously involved.

She had been accustomed to prescribe for patients and at this she had gained for herself an enviable reputation; but here is a difficult form of acute heart trouble, unknown to the medical profession as such. I once heard a physician say, that a doctor should never shake his head, and say: "I cannot do anything more." Then he added: "I always do something for a sufferer, no matter how hopeless the case." Bravo! Doctor. Prescribe anyhow. Make a new record in therapeutics.

This much may be said as to particulars: I went South to my work, and could only reach my physician through correspondence. This naturally prolonged the diagnosis, though I tried to give the exact, and correct symptoms. The doctor, however, did not seem anxious to venture her reputation on guess work, or, at long range. But all is well that ends well, and the business once started had to come to an end. And so, on August 1, 1914, while the cables and wireless stations were informing the world that Germany had opened war on Belgium, and that all Europe was becoming involved; at noonday, in Allen Church, Philadelphia, Bishop Tanner pronounced the words:

"I now declare that they are man and wife together, in the name of the Father, and of the Son, and of the Holy Ghost; Amen."

This day marks the fifth anniversary. As I write these lines I hear the voice of our Theodosia, a rollicking "Tom-boy girl," three and a half years old; decidely precocious; naturally spoiled. But she has a wise mother. "At evening time it shall be light." The little "Divine gift" is a ray of light. Such a ray as generally comes in the morning; but, if at "evening time," all the more glorious and cheering. Light at evening! "Lead kindly light," until the day is quite passed; and then, "Amid the encircling gloom," lead thou me on.